50 hikes

in

Central Pennsylvania

Day Hikes and Backpacking Trips

Third Edition

TOM THWAITES

Photographs by the author

Backcountry Publications

Woodstock, Vermont

7-22-97

An Invitation to the Reader
Over time, trails can be rerouted and signs and landmarks altered. If you find that changes have occurred on the routes described in this book, please let us know so that corrections may be made in future editions. The author and publisher also welcome other comments and suggestions. Address all correspondence to:

Editor, 50 Hikes Series
Backcountry Publications
PO Box 175
Woodstock, VT 05091-0175

Library of Congress Cataloging-in-Publication Data
Thwaites, Tom.
    Fifty hikes in central Pennsylvania : day hikes and backpacking trips / Tom Thwaites; photographs by the author. — 3rd ed.
        p. cm.
    ISBN 0-88150-353-3
    1. Hiking—Pennsylvania—Guidebooks. 2. Backpacking—Pennsylvania—Guidebooks. 3. Trails—Pennsylvania—Guidebooks. 4. Pennsylvania—Guidebooks.   I. Title.
    GV199.42.P4T48   1995   95-10000
    796.5'1'09748—dc20   CIP

© 1979, 1985, 1995 by Thomas T. Thwaites

Published by Backcountry Publications,
a division of The Countryman Press, Inc.,
PO Box 175, Woodstock, Vermont 05091–0175.

Printed in the United States of America

Photograph on p. 97 by Terry Smith, Bald Eagle State Forest
Text and cover design by Glenn Suokko
Trail overlays by Richard Widhu
Cover photograph by the author

DEDICATION

To the memory of my niece, Laura Braun, who would
have enjoyed all these hikes.

ACKNOWLEDGMENTS

Many of the hikes in this book were suggested by members of the Keystone Trails Association or by employees of the Pennsylvania Bureau of Forestry. I thank all those trail workers who build and maintain hiking trails in Penn's Woods.

I am particularly grateful to Ralph Seeley, Rich Scanlon, Doug Fowler, Jim Lipko, Gene Huston, Woody Schwartz, Bob Lee, Mark Dowd, John Eastlake, and all the other companions who hiked with me in the course of this revision. I am particularly grateful to my wife, Barbara, who served as hiking companion, driver, typist, and editor.

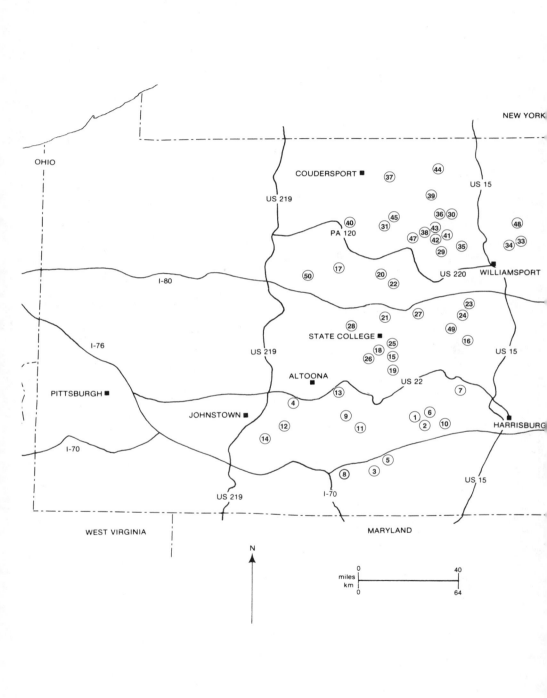

CONTENTS

INTRODUCTION

SCRANTON ■

I-80

NEW JERSEY

I-76

PHILADELPHIA ■

DELAWARE

NORTH DISTRICT

BACKPACKING TRIPS

Map Symbols

— main trail

- - - side trail

Ⓟ parking

⇧⇧ view

⊼ picnic area

△ campsite

INTRODUCTION

Between the heavily used Appalachian Trail in Pennsylvania's southeast and the widely known Allegheny National Forest in its opposite corner lies a broad but often ignored expanse of Penn's Woods with some of the best hiking in the Northeast.

Here, in central Pennsylvania, little-used trails take you along ridges, through valleys, and across plateaus. The views from this region's endless mountains are pleasing and varied, even though none of the peaks aspires to timberline, let alone a snowcap. On one side of a ridge prosperous farms may checker the valley, and on the other, waves of the forest sea roll unbroken to the horizon. While other trails in Pennsylvania are being loved to death by increasing numbers of hikers, many trails in this area are slowly disappearing under the relentless growth of huckleberry, mountain laurel, and scrub oak.

The total length of these central Pennsylvania trails, which are mostly on public land, is estimated to exceed that of the entire Appalachian Trail. For a region surrounded on three sides by urbanized areas, this is a remarkable resource. A system of wild and natural areas totaling 68,000 hectares has been established within Pennsylvania's state forests. This book contains hikes in 17 of these areas.

The Penn's Woods described in this book are long on silence, solitude, and stories. Pennsylvania probably has more ghost towns than Colorado, but since wood doesn't last here as it does in the desert mountains of the West, they are not as visible or dramatic. Old roads, railroad grades, and log slides lie along many hikes, remnants of a once populous and productive era.

If you are a hiker, I urge you to switch from overused trails elsewhere to underused trails in Penn's Woods. If you are not hiking yet, I hope to convince you the only way to see and experience Penn's Woods is to get out of your car and back on your feet. When you have the hiking habit try backpacking—you will be free to roam Penn's Woods with a maximum of independence.

TRAILS

These hikes cover a variety of trails. Some are blazed and maintained on a regular basis; others are merely identified by signs at intersections and depend on use to keep them clear. The system of marked trails on public lands expanded rapidly during the 1970s, and some trails are still being built. Most trail work today, however, consists of relocations designed to reduce road walking; to permit a more scenic, historic, or pleasing route; or perhaps just to avoid private land. (These relocations, of course, may cause a section of trail to differ from its description here.)

FOOTWEAR

Through-hikers on the Appalachian Trail invariably report that Pennsylvania has the rockiest part of the 3200-km-long route. Proper hiking boots are a must for many of these hikes. I recommend medium-weight leather boots, 15 centimeters high, with lugged soles and waterproofing. Leather boots have largely been replaced today by glorified sneakers made of plastic and mere scraps of leather. While cheaper, such boots do not last as long as leather ones and cannot be resoled. Only if you pay almost as much as you would for leather are you likely to get a satisfactory pair.

When you buy boots be sure to fit them over the socks you wear hiking—a thin, inner pair and a thick, mostly wool, outer pair. Some hikes are identified in the text as negotiable with rubber-soled walking shoes. Children may get by with sneakers on such trails but adults wearing sneakers invite sprained ankles.

CLOTHING AND EQUIPMENT

On summer hikes the task is keeping cool, so shorts and short-sleeved shirts are best. Remember that cotton will keep you cooler than synthetics. The difference between a walker and a hiker is a pack. In a frameless day pack you should carry no more than 5 or 6 kilograms of gear, which should include the following:

1. Water. Fill your canteen at home or from another tested water source. All springs and streams should be considered contaminated and water from them should be filtered or treated with iodine.
2. Food. You should include a candy bar, bag of gorp, tin of pemmican, fruitcake, or other emergency food, as well as your lunch.
3. Rain parka or poncho. Rain is inevitable in Pennsylvania. Be ready for it.
4. Windbreaker, or wool shirt or sweater. You should always be prepared for cold. A Gore-Tex rain parka can double.
5. Pocket knife with can opener.

6. Small first-aid kit with bandages, moleskin, aspirin, and first-aid cream.
7. Flashlight. Hiking a trail in the dark is no fun, and darkness comes early on a cloudy November day.
8. Map and compass. These are optional on most hikes but may prove reassuring on some, such as Splash Dam Hollow.
9. Miscellaneous. Insect repellent (seasonal); toilet paper (always); identification guides to birds, trees, or wildflowers; extra roll of film; and spare spectacles all come in handy. In addition, a brimmed hat keeps the sun off ears and neck, reduces areas vulnerable to insect attack, and keeps rain off glasses.

Hiking during spring and fall is more enjoyable than in summer. The insects are gone, it's cooler, and you find wildflowers or colored leaves along the trail. In these seasons wool shows its miraculous qualities. Long pants and a long-sleeved shirt of light wool or polypropylene keep you comfortable even in bad weather. Again, you want extra clothing in your pack in case of rain or real cold.

Winter hiking calls for shirt, pants, and underwear of wool or polypropylene. You will be surprised at how warm you can be on winter hikes—as long as you keep moving. However, you need a parka or sweater once you stop. A sitting pad of 6-millimeter ensolite is welcome if you rest amid snow and ice. Winter is no time to leave your canteen behind. The dry air leaves you thirsty. Don't forget gaiters to close the gap between boot tops and pant cuffs.

BACKPACKING

A real treat in Penn's Woods is backpacking on state forest lands. Under new regulations, camping permits will be required. Call the relevant state forest office during normal business hours. If time allows, they will mail your permit to you. If not, they will leave your permit near their front door for you to pick up on your way to the trailhead. They can also fax it to you. As of this writing, there is no fee for a camping permit.

Be aware that the five hikes designated herein for backpacking are lengthy trips. For your first backpacking experience select a day hike with an overnight option (see Hikes 14, 20, 21, 22, 23, 25, 33, 34, 36, 38, 39, 40, 43, and 45).

You need a frame pack with a padded hipbelt, a good sleeping bag, and a tent or tarp—there are few shelters on these trails. The padded hipbelt, a revolution in backpacks, transfers the weight of your pack from your shoulders to your hips, thus bypassing your back. Packs, bags, and tents are big-ticket items but it's usually possible to rent them if you're not ready to buy.

Here are a few tips on sleeping bags. First, your best bet is a mummy bag. It is warmer than a rectangular bag of the same weight. Some mummy bags are confining, but others are cut generously; you should find a style that suits. Second, do not feel you must have expensive down-filled items. Down gear is necessary in the dry desert mountains of the West, where almost all precipitation comes as snow and the cold and stormy weather warrants extra protection. In Pennsylvania's climate you can wear outer garments that are less expensive and still provide warmth. Down also has two related drawbacks—when wet it ceases to insulate, and it is impossible to dry in the field. Look for Polarguard and Lite Loft; they insulate when wet and are relatively easy to dry and so are better suited to the temperate rain forests of Appalachia.

For cooking, small backpacking stoves are superior to the old-fashioned campfire. They are a minimal fire hazard, don't leave soot on your pots, and don't deplete the firewood supply. Furthermore, they heat food in a fraction of the time it takes to find firewood, cut it, and begin the fire, and they function in wet weather, when all the wood will be wet anyway.

There's no need to use expensive, freeze-dried food for a weekend or 3-day backpacking trip. Get supermarket dried foods and mixes, such as macaroni and cheese, soups, tuna, hamburger and other helpers, along with oatmeal, cheese, and concentrated foods. Small cans of tuna, ham, or other meat are suitable but remember to carry out empty cans after washing them to prevent your pack from stinking. Also, opaque foils contain a layer of unburnable aluminum and must be carried out.

For a week-long trip you definitely need some freeze-dried or dehydrated food to keep pack weight down to 25 percent of body weight. An alternative may be a food drop or cache halfway along the route.

Before your first trip set up the tent in your own yard to make sure you have all its parts. Make sure the stove works properly too. Boil some water and compare the time it takes to the stated value for your model—but remember to do this outside. Never operate your stove inside a building.

SAFETY IN THE WOODS

Compared to the risk of an auto accident driving to and from the trailhead, the woods are safe. Still, there are hazards in the woods not present in urban areas.

Bears and rattlesnakes do not constitute real hazards. Bears are hunted in Pennsylvania and are consequently very shy. Count yourself lucky if you catch even a glimpse of one. And what do you do if you meet a rattlesnake? Surprisingly, the answer is "Don't pick it up!" Almost all snake bites are to hands or arms.

The real hazards in the woods are either microbial or inanimate. Lightning is a hazard to hikers, as ridges are frequently hit. Look for evidence of strikes, such as a furrow high up on a tree trunk, where the bark has been blasted off. If you are caught on a ridge in a thunderstorm, move down the side to a uniformly tall stand of trees.

Lyme disease is a new threat to the health of outdoorspeople. It is caused by a spirochete and is transmitted by the bite of the deer tick *(Ixodes dammini).* Most bites are from the nymph of the deer tick, which is about the size of the period at the end of this sentence, so your chances of seeing it are zero. Lyme disease can occur wherever deer are found. Ticks climb vegetation to catch rides on passing animals, including hikers. Beware of grassy areas and keep to the middle of the trail. If possible, take a shower after your hike. The water may sluice off any unattached ticks.

Symptoms of Lyme disease imitate those of many other diseases such as flu, meningitis, encephalitis, cardiac arrythmias, arthritis, multiple sclerosis, as well as Alzheimer's disease and other dementias. There is still no reliable medical test for Lyme disease. A few years ago it was widely unrecognized but today it may be over-diagnosed. Considering the number of people at risk there is precious little funding for research on Lyme disease.

If you find a tick attached to you, remove it with tweezers or blunt forceps. Grasp the tick as close as possible to where the mouth parts enter your skin. Pull steadily, taking care not to crush the tick or break off the mouth parts. Save the tick in a small bottle or plastic bag, as your doctor may decide to put you on a course of antibiotics if it turns out to be a deer tick.

Ticks are most active in spring and summer but can be encountered even on a warm day in winter. The only time I've seen a deer tick (it was an adult) was in November. The first line of protection against ticks is clothing. If you wear long pants, tuck them into your socks or boots and spray them with Permanone tick repellent. If you find long pants insufferably hot and wear shorts instead, then apply DEET to your bare legs. DEET is found in many commercial repellents and you should use a relatively low concentration for direct application to your skin. This application may drive ticks down into your socks, so keep checking there. Don't crush a tick with your fingers as this will get tick fluids on your skin.

The first sign of Lyme disease is one or more red rashes, which may or may not occur on the site of the tick bite. The good news is that these rashes are present in at least 80 percent of cases. The bad news is that they may be located under your arms, behind your knees, or on your back where you can't see them without a mirror or a friend. Lyme disease is treatable with antibiotics at all stages but there is a premium on early treatment. If you think you may have been exposed, call the American Lyme Disease Foundation (1-800-876-LYME) for the name of a physician in your area who is experienced in treating Lyme disease.

Another microbial hazard is giardiasis, caused by a protozoan about 10 microns in size. All unprotected and untested water sources must be considered contaminated with this parasite. Submicron water filters such as MSR Waterworks, PUR Water Purifier, and First Need—or treatment with iodine—are appropriate for backpacking trips; for day trips simply fill your canteen at home. Boiling water to purify it in the field is recommended only by those who haven't tried it.

Don't hike during bear or deer hunting seasons in November and December.

Hypothermia stalks Penn's Woods for the unwary whenever the temperature is below 10 degrees C—at least 6 months of every year. Hypothermia is best avoided by dressing right. Cold rain or wet snow call for rain gear, nowadays usually Gore-Tex. Wool or polypropylene will keep you warm even when they're wet. It helps to wear layers so you can remove outer garments when you are breathing hard, and put them on again when you stop to rest. Eating right can also forestall hypothermia. Don't skip breakfast before a hike and do carry snacks such as fruitcake or chocolate bars in your pack. Get a victim of hypothermia out of any wet cotton clothes and into dry clothes or a sleeping bag. If shelter is not immediately available, build two fires, one on each side of the victim.

With reasonable precautions we can hike and enjoy Pennsylvania's beautiful woods.

ABOUT THIS BOOK

The 50 hikes in this book were selected for their wide range of hiking experiences and to introduce hikers to Pennsylvania's wild and natural areas as well as its organized trails. They range from walks that take less than an hour to a week-long backpacking trip. I have made every effort to devise circuit hikes, and those that cannot be looped are included as short out-and-back hikes or longer car shuttle hikes. All of these hikes have been field checked for the third edition. Parts of the Lost Turkey Trail cross private land. This is, however, a blazed and maintained trail, and landowners have given permission for trail use by the public. I hope hikers' conduct allows this happy situation to continue.

The hikes are distributed over three areas in the central portion of the state. The south district runs from the Mason-Dixon Line north to US 22. The central

district extends from US 22 north to PA 120 and US 220. The north district stretches from that line to the New York border.

The hikes are divided into introductory, or half-day hikes, and day hikes. The dividing line between these types is 3 hours, or 8 km. Backpacking trips require 2 or more days.

The summary headings for each hike list distance, hiking time, vertical rise, highlights, and relevant maps. These headings should help you decide which hikes match your capabilities and the time available. Distance is the total distance hiked when you complete the described route. Most hikes can be shortened, and some include directions for specific shortcuts. This book gives hiking distances in metric units; driving directions to the trailheads are given in miles.

The trailheads for some hikes are on so-called state routes (SR, followed by 4 digits). These roads are paved but their quality is one level below that of regular state highways (PA, followed by 3 digits). Inconspicuous signs bearing the state route number can be found at the ends of each road, and at important intersections along the way.

Each hike in this book, with the exception of the Golden Eagle Trail, was measured with a 2-meter measuring wheel manufactured by the Rolatape Corporation. Distances measured with a wheel are more reliable than those obtained with a pedometer.

Walking times are set by SOAP (standard old-age pace) and do not take into account extended lunch stops or other breaks. Novice hikers may not match these times but with experience the young can easily surpass them.

Vertical rise is the total amount of climbing along the route. It may occur all in one climb, in which case it is the difference between the lowest and highest points on the route. But it may and frequently does occur over several climbs. If there are any descents between these climbs then the vertical rise noted for the hike will exceed the difference between the lowest and highest points on the hike. Vertical rise, which is listed in both feet and meters, can turn even the shortest hike into a real challenge. A topographic map showing the route and landmarks is included with each hike.

If you find yourself becoming an avid hiker, I recommend you join a hiking club. You can find the nearest one through the Keystone Trails Association. A hiking club allows you to meet others who share your enthusiasm—and to help maintain the trails in Penn's Woods. It is a well-kept secret that maintaining a hiking trail is one of the most satisfying outdoor activities known. Happy hiking!

OTHER HELPFUL INFORMATION

• *Pennsylvania Hiking Trails,* 11th edition, 1993. Published by the Keystone Trails Association, PO Box 251, Cogan Station, PA 17728. Mid State Trail map and guide sets can also be ordered from the Keystone Trails Association. Write for current prices.
• *The Short Hiker,* 2nd edition, by Jean Aron, 1994. The 31 hikes in this book are all near State College.
• *Short Hikes in Pennsylvania's Grand Canyon,* Vol. 1, 2nd edition, by Chuck Dillon, 1993. Published by Pine Creek Press. The 56 hikes in this book are all in Tioga State Forest.
• *Roadside Geology of Pennsylvania,* by Bradford B. Van Diver, 1990. Published by Mountain Press Publishing Company. This book will add greatly to your enjoyment of Pennsylvania's exciting geology. A whole lot happens when continents collide, and you can see much of it from Pennsylvania's trails.
• Topographic maps are available from the U.S. Geological Survey, Map Distribution Center, Federal Center, Box 25286, Denver, CO 80225, and in most backpacking stores ($4 per map).
• For a copy of the official Pennsylvania Transportation Map showing most organized hiking trails as well as state forests, gamelands, and parks, write to: Travel Development Bureau, Pennsylvania Department of Commerce, Harrisburg, PA 17120.
• The umbrella hiking organization in Penn's Woods is the Keystone Trails Association, PO Box 251, Cogan Station, PA 17728-0251. Membership, as of this writing, is still only $6 a year but will rise to $9 in October 1995. The four yearly issues of the *KTA Newsletter* are alone worth several times the fee. Updates for hikes in this book will be given in the "Hiker Alert" column of the *KTA Newsletter.*

SOUTH DISTRICT

1

Path Valley Railroad Tunnel

Distance: 2.1 km (1.3 miles)

Time: 45 minutes

Vertical Rise: 90 meters (300 ft)

Highlights: Uncompleted railroad tunnel

Map: USGS 7.5' Blairs Mills

On this short hike you visit the ruins of two narrow-gauge railroads. The ruins, in the vicinity of Big Spring State Park in Tuscarora State Forest, are all that remain of the hope and determination of railroad officials and the hard work of laborers at the turn of the century.

The first remnant is an incomplete railroad tunnel intended to carry the Path Valley Railroad through Conococheague Mountain into Path Valley. In 1893 the Path Valley Railroad was chartered and began construction of the grade and the tunnel, which was to be 800 meters long. With great confidence in its surveyors, the company started construction from both sides of the moun-

tain. The mountainside was covered with a deep layer of loose and broken rock on the west, or Path Valley, side. Digging never reached the solid rock.

On the east side, which you visit, workers hit hard rock immediately. The forces that produced these folded mountains hundreds of millions of years ago also metamorphosed the rock into flint. The flint resisted blasting with black powder and progress was slow. Initial efforts to dig the tunnel ended in 1895 when unpaid workmen abandoned the project. In 1910 a final effort was made to complete it but the total distance tunneled was only 37 meters.

In comparison, the Perry Lumber Company's railroad, whose grade you also travel, was a success. The company purchased a single Climax locomotive, acquired 19,000 acres of western Perry County, and in the space of 4 years (1901–1905) cut the entire tract. The company appears to have been relatively efficient. According to authorities on Pennsylvania logging, many other operations left bark and hardwood to rot on the hillsides, but Perry sold the bark to tanneries and used the leftover hardwood for barrel staves and chemical wood. The company's lands were eventually purchased by the state and became

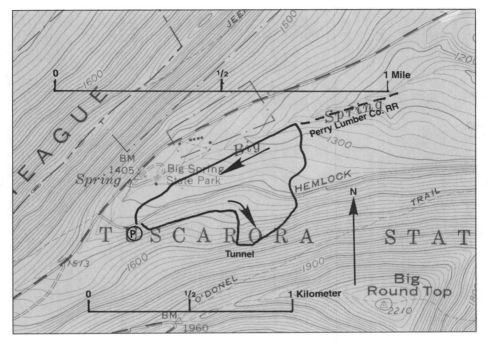

part of the present Tuscarora State Forest.

To reach Big Spring State Park, drive 5.8 miles southwest from New Germantown on PA 274, or 4.8 miles northeast from the junction of PA 274 and PA 75 near Doylesburg. Turn off PA 274 at Hemlock Road, which is just west of the main parking area for the state park. Cross a culvert and bear left into a small parking area. The hike, for which walking shoes are sufficient, begins at the display case containing information on the railroads and the trail.

The blue-blazed trail quickly climbs to the rough end of a Path Valley Railroad grade. The railroad may have been for use by geared locomotives, as the average grade from New Germantown to the tunnel entrance was to be 3.7 percent. Rod-type steam locomotives would have had considerable difficulty on this grade. As you proceed, the grade becomes more finished and then ends abruptly. You then descend a set of steps and bear right uphill. As you look ahead you see the end of another grade (the gap between these two was to be filled with rock blasted from the tunnel) and on climbing you find it cuts into the mountainside. The cut is partially filled with fallen rocks and trees have grown among them.

The tunnel opening, barely visible over the rocks, reveals relatively little rockfall inside, but beware of exploring it as the footing is wet and slippery. In wet weather the tunnel may fill with water dammed by the fallen rocks outside.

You continue by following the trail down off the fill at the end of the cut, crossing Hemlock Road, and then winding downhill to the old Perry Lumber Company railroad grade. To the right the grade heads down the valley to New Germantown, but the trail turns left and leads to the track's end. The company operated a sawmill at this railhead but

Old railroad grade

little evidence of it remains.

You soon reenter Big Spring State Park and bear left around a picnic shelter built by the Civilian Conservation Corps in the 1930s. Follow the trail around the main part of the park and head back to the small parking area and your car.

Other hiking opportunities near Big Spring State Park include the Iron Horse Trail, which follows the Perry Lumber Company railroad grade to the east (Hike 6); and the Hemlocks Natural Area, which is 4 miles farther up Hemlock Road (Hike 2).

2

Hemlocks Natural Area

Distance: 2.7 km (1.4 miles)	
Time: 1 hour	
Vertical Rise: 120 meters (400 ft)	
Highlights: Virgin timber	
Map: USGS 7.5' Doylesburg	

A 50-hectare stand of old-growth hemlock along Patterson Run in Tuscarora State Forest distinguishes this hike. The trees in this stand are estimated to be 300 to 500 years old, and we can only speculate on their survival in the midst of logging country. The brittle hemlock generally brings a low price, and these particular trees are in a steep canyon between Hemlock Mountain and Little Round Top. The trees' low marketability and the difficulty of felling, stripping, and removing them may have influenced the Perry Lumber Company to bypass them during their operations here from 1901 to 1905.

The hemlocks approach the maximum size for the species—around 40 meters high and 185 cm in diameter. The tallest tree measured here is 37 meters high and the thickest is 130 cm in diameter. This area has had a special significance since 1931, when the hemlock was designated Pennsylvania's state tree.

To reach the Hemlocks Natural Area, drive 5.8 miles southwest from New Germantown on PA 274, or 4.8 miles northeast from the junction of PA 274 and PA 75 near Doylesburg. Turn off PA 274 onto Hemlock Road and drive for 4 miles to a small parking lot. (Along the last 1.5 miles you can see some of the large trees of the natural area.)

Several hiking routes go through the area but the one you take requires a minimum amount of road walking and no backtracking. Walking shoes are adequate although the trail is rocky in places. From the parking lot you follow the wood-chipped path downhill just under 130 meters to a bridge over Patterson Run. Turn left at the junction just across the bridge, and recross Patterson Run on another bridge. The Hemlock Trail becomes rough and rocky as it goes downstream. Bear right at any forks, following this trail across Patterson Run again and up to a junction with the Rim and Laurel Trails at 1.1 km. Turn sharply right onto the Rim Trail; there are some fine views

Tall trees in the natural area

of the hemlocks farther up the slope.

The Rim Trail leads you back to the junction at the first bridge you crossed; you could truncate your hike now by taking the wood-chipped path back to your car. On this hike, however, turn left, heading upstream on the Hemlock Trail, which crosses the run twice more on bridges before moving up to Hemlock Road. Here you take a right turn and walk 400 meters back to your car.

Additional hiking opportunities can be found on the Tuscarora Trail, which is just 500 meters farther up Hemlock Road.

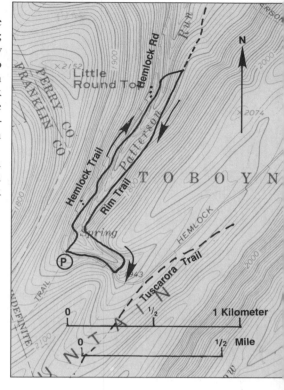

3

Cowans Gap State Park

Distance: 5.9 km (3.7 miles)

Time: 2¼ hours

Vertical Rise: 180 meters (600 ft)

Highlights: Wind gap

Maps: USGS 7.5' McConnellsburg; park map

Cowans Gap, a wind gap through Tuscarora Mountain, is located in Buchanan State Forest. A wind gap is formed when a stream that originally flowed across the grain of the ridge-and-valley region is captured by a stream that flows with the grain. This happens because the latter can erode its valley faster than the former can cut a water gap through the mountains. Here at Cowans Gap, Little Aughwick Creek's capture of the stream now flowing north out of Allens Valley must have been quite recent, in geologic terms. Prior to this capture, Allens Valley drained east through this gap in the Tuscarora Ridge.

You reach Cowans Gap State Park by driving north for 6.4 miles from US 30 on Aughwick Road; by driving south 6.9 miles from US 522 on Burnt Cabins Road; or by driving northwest 3.1 miles from PA 75 on Richmond Road. Once in the park, follow signs to the office, where you can get a booklet describing the hike's points of interest, and then continue on to park at the end of picnic area lot 5. Despite some wet spots you can get by with walking shoes on this short hike.

To begin, walk down this same road toward the bridge over Little Aughwick Creek, but just before the bridge, turn left onto the Plessinger Trail. The Plessinger is marked with red blazes. Follow the trail for 2.0 km as it goes upstream between Camping Area A on your left and the creek on your right. At some places the trail divides into several routes. Some follow the stream bank more closely than others, but they all rejoin after a bit.

The black gum is a common tree along the trail. Its leaves are not distinctive but the bark of larger trees is deeply furrowed and strongly resembles an alligator hide. The tree's wood is very tough, and in the fall its leaves turn a brilliant scarlet.

In March of 1993 Cowans Gap was hit by a windstorm. The ground was still soaked from the spring thaw and a great many trees were blown over, blocking

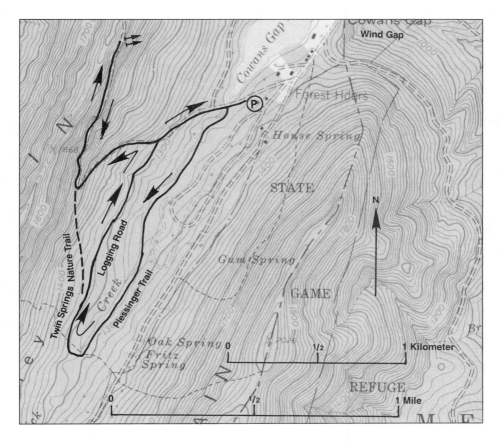

trails in and around the park. As a result, a 400-hectare salvage cut is underway to the west of Little Aughwick Creek. Since all the logs on that side of the creek belong to the logger, western trails, including the Twin Springs and others, can't be reopened until the salvage operation is completed sometime in 1995. Then volunteers will reopen these trails.

In the meantime you can complete this hike by following a logging road. Turn right on the blue-blazed Twin Springs Nature Trail and cross the footbridge over Little Aughwick Creek. At the far end of the footbridge bear right, and then left. Crawl over, through, and around blowdowns to reach the logging

road above, where you turn right. Continue on the logging road to Knobsville Road and make a left. Follow Knobsville Road uphill to an overlook of Cowans Gap and Lake. A platform at the overlook affords a view through Cowans Gap into Path Valley.

To end your hike retrace your steps down Knobsville Road past a vehicle gate and across the creek to the parking lot.

You might also want to check with the park office on the progress of the salvage cut. When the Twin Springs Trail is reopened you can follow it, rather than the logging road, to its intersection with Knobsville Road.

The Twin Springs Trail is notable for

Cowans Lake in the gap

its charcoal flats, or hearths, and its American chestnut shoots. The charcoal produced here was presumably used to smelt iron ore at Richmond Furnace over in Path Valley.

The American chestnut has bladelike leaves with notched edges that strongly resemble the smooth-edged leaves of the chestnut oak. At the turn of the century every other hardwood in the Appalachians from Maine to Georgia was a chestnut. The ideal forest tree, its nuts could be eaten by humans and animals. Its wood was used for everything from fence posts to window frames. After logging, chestnut stumps sprouted again and the new trees grew rapidly. However, early in this century the trees contracted a fungal blight from abroad and were virtually eliminated. Today the stumps continue to send up shoots, some of which bear burrs before they are again felled by the chestnut blight. The trees' siege is probably the greatest ecological disaster ever to hit North America.

Additional hiking opportunities at Cowans Gap State Park can be found on its Tuscarora Trail.

4

Allegheny Portage Railroad

Distance: 7.0 km (4.4 miles)

Time: 3 hours

Vertical Rise: 175 meters (575 ft)

Highlights: Historic ruins

Map: USGS 7.5' Cresson

Don't be put off by the wood-chip surfacing on several of the trails on this hike. A great deal of history lies along them, and they may even hold lessons about today's technology.

The portage railway was the 1830s' solution to getting a canal over a mountain. It carried canal traffic from the head of navigation on the Juniata River over Allegheny Mountain to the head of navigation on the Conemaugh River. Today we realize that Pennsylvania officials should have built a proper railroad from Philadelphia to Pittsburgh to compete with the Erie and Chesapeake and Ohio Canals. But the railroads of that day were puny—they couldn't climb the grades carrying the weight that loaded canal boats could. The building of the Pennsylvania Canal was the prudent choice, but the rapid development of railroads made the canal-and-portage system obsolete within 20 years of its completion—not even long enough to pay off the bonds that had been sold to finance the project. Nevertheless, canals did cut the shipping time from Philadelphia to Pittsburgh from over 3 weeks by wagon to only 3½ days.

The Allegheny Portage Railroad system built to get the canal over the Allegheny Mountains included an ascent of 420 meters at the end of the Juniata Canal at Hollidaysburg. Stationary steam engines pulled the railroad cars up a series of 10 inclines divided equally on both sides of the summit. (There are no weight restrictions on a stationary engine and also no traction problems.) The inclines had grades from 4 to 6 percent, but unlike those for a railroad, they had to be straight. Hemp ropes were used to pull the cars initially, but incidences of runaway loads resulted in a switch to steel cables. On levels between inclines, cars could be pulled by horses, but the animals were soon replaced by steam locomotives. In the 1840s the Allegheny Portage Railroad was one of the engineering

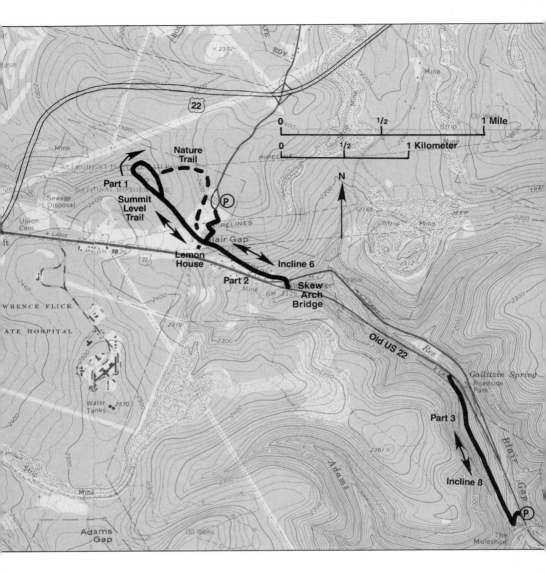

wonders of the world, but by 1855 it had been abandoned as obsolete.

You can reach the first of several hiking trails at the Allegheny Portage Railroad National Historic Site by driving to the Gallitzin exit of US 22. Turn south and drive 0.9 mile to the parking lot at the new visitors center. Ordinary walking shoes are fine for this hike. After inspecting the exhibits, start your hike from the breezeway in front of the visitors center.

Follow the boardwalk down to a trail junction at Engine House 6. Turn right and inspect the engine house. The steam engine here pulled canal boats up Incline 6. Then continue west past the

Reconstructed tracks on Incline 6 at Allegheny Portage

Lemon House. This was once the home of Samuel Lemon, who, by selling coal and timber to the Portage Railroad and food to workmen and passengers, became one of the richest men in Cambria County.

As you continue walking west on the Summit Level Trail notice the stone ties or sleepers that have been exposed in the cuts. The fairly deep cuts were made by hand. Unlike wooden ties, the sleepers were unconnected and did not maintain the separation between the rails. Despite their great mass (about 200 kg each) the sleepers moved and settled, so derailments were frequent.

Keeping left at the trail junction you soon pass a stone culvert under the old grade. Notice its keystone arch. How elegant compared to the concrete pipe used to carry the same intermittent stream under the return trail! Soon you pass two trails on the left leading to a picnic area. Continue on the Summit Level Trail across the old railroad bed in a loop. After a bit you rejoin the main trail; retrace your steps back to the Engine House. Or you can vary your return by taking the Summit Nature Trail back to the Engine House. The Nature Trail will increase your hike by 2 km and is certainly worth the additional time. A pamphlet describing the Summit Nature Trail is available at the visitors center.

The second part of this hike also begins at Engine House 6. Now you walk east, downhill, past a reconstructed portion of Incline 6. Note the primitive design of the Portage Railroad, which required two full sets of rails rather than a single set with a bypass halfway down. Farther downhill you jog left across a side road; a short distance beyond you come to the westbound lanes of Old US 22. Use great care in crossing to arrive at the Skew Arch Bridge and the end of this trail. The bridge is the site of a pre-existing wagon road that crossed over the Portage Railroad and continued to carry traffic until 1922. You now retrace your steps to the visitors center.

The third part of this hike, 2.7 km long, takes you up Incline 8. You need your car to reach it. Drive back to US 22 and turn west. At the next exit—the Summit interchange—turn east on Old US 22. Drive 3.5 miles, passing the Lemon House, and proceed downhill. Just before the new Portage Railroad bridge (also known as the Muleshoe Curve) park as best you can on the right.

The new Portage Railroad, built in 1855, was a last-gasp attempt to save the canal system. It replaced the entire system of levels and inclines with a conventional railroad, but lasted only 2 years. In 1857, the state sold the entire system to the Pennsylvania Railroad. This bridge continued in use until the 1980s but the tracks have now been pulled up.

To reach Incline 8, follow an obvious dirt road from the parking area. After 200 meters turn right, to the start of Incline 8. With a vertical rise of 94 meters and a grade of 6 percent, this is the highest and steepest of the 10 inclines.

The excavated ruins of Engine House 8 lie at the top of the incline. Continue on this level for another 500 meters to where it has been destroyed by the eastbound lanes of Old US 22. At the very end you can see 15 sleepers. Indeed, most of Incline 7 and the level above it also were destroyed by the highway—a pity, given the spectacular nature of Blair Gap between here and Incline 6.

Incline 7 may well have inspired Charles Dickens's account of his passage over the Portage Railroad in 1842. "Occasionally the rails are laid upon the extreme verge of a giddy precipice; and looking down from the carriage window the traveller gazes sheer down, without a stone or scrap of fence between, into the mountain depths below . . . It is very pretty travelling thus, at a rapid pace along the heights of the mountain in a keen wind, to look down into a valley full of light and softness; catching glimpses, through the tree tops, of scattered cabins; children running to the doors; dogs bursting out to bark, whom we could see without hearing; terrified pigs scampering homewards; families sitting out in their rude gardens; cows gazing upward with a stupid indifference; men in their shirtsleeves looking on at their unfinished houses, planning out tomorrow's work; and we riding onward, high above them, like a whirlwind."

Once again, retrace your steps and return to your car.

5

Tuscarora Ridge Trail

Distance: 7.4 km (4.6 miles)

Time: 2¼ hours

Vertical Rise: 125 meters (400 ft)

Highlights: Views

Map: USGS 7.5' Fannettsburg

Wild azalea is uncommon in Penn's Woods but thickets dotted with this delicate flower abound along this trail on Tuscarora Ridge. The flowers are in bloom the first or second week in May, an ideal time for this hike. This section of one of Pennsylvania's longest trails also boasts excellent views of Path Valley to the east and Burnt Cabins, Cove Mountain, and the southern end of Shade Mountain to the west. The footway is the best along any ridgetop trail in the state. The crushed sandstone, typically used by the Civilian Conservation Corps, indicates the trail may have been built by the Corps in the 1930s. The trail is also unusual because it runs along the top of the ridge rather than straight up one side and down the

other. Hiking boots are in order for this rocky trail.

From Exit 14 on the Pennsylvania Turnpike drive south on PA 75 for 2.1 miles to the town of Fannettsburg. Then bear right on Burnt Cabins Road for 2.3 miles to the top of Tuscarora Ridge and the trailhead. Or drive 2.8 miles from US 522 in Burnt Cabins on the same road toward Fannettsburg. Park on the north side of the road or on the south side just west of the crest.

Orange blazes mark the trail; the large white blazes here mark the edge of Buchanan State Forest land. Begin walking up the jeep road along a pole line, but then immediately swing left through the woods. At 400 meters a large rock to the right of the trail offers a view over Path Valley and Fannettsburg. Path Valley is named for the Tuscarora tribe path that traversed it. A more extensive view by a large and picturesque white pine lies 200 meters farther on. At 1.2 km there is a power line across the ridge.

Proceed along the trail for a series of views both east and west. Farther along you can see the turnpike, first to the west, and then to the east as well. Over the years the Tuscarora Trail has been traveled so much that the end of the old Civilian Conservation Corps footway is no

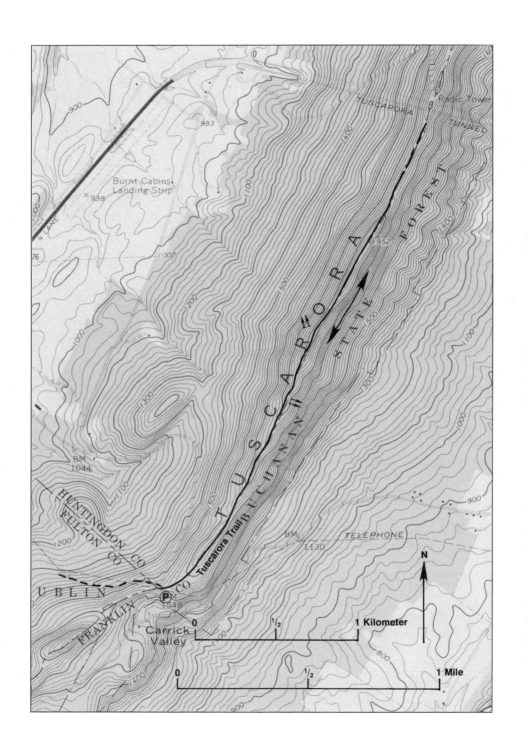

Wild azalea

longer apparent; after 3.7 km, though, you will reach a fence around a fire tower above the Tuscarora Tunnel of the Pennsylvania Turnpike. Turn around here and retrace your steps to your car.

Additional hiking opportunities can be found at nearby Cowans Gap State Park (Hike 3).

6

Iron Horse Trail

Distance: 7.4 km (4.6 miles)

Time: 2½ hours

Vertical Rise: 210 meters (690 ft)

Highlights: Old narrow-gauge railroad grade

Maps: USGS 7.5' Blairs Mills; Blain

Steam railroads played a major role in the development of Pennsylvania. The Iron Horse Trail, located in the western part of Perry County, consists largely of the abandoned grades of two such railroads. To one side of PA 274, the trail follows the grade of a narrow-gauge logging railroad built and used by the Perry Lumber Company (1901–1905). On the other side of the highway the trail follows the almost completed Path Valley Railroad grade (1893–1910). The Path Valley was to provide common carrier rail service to the valley beyond Conococheague Mountain. (See Hike 1 for more about these two turn-of-the-century railroads.) The narrow-gauge East Broad Top Railroad provided similar

service a couple of valleys to the west and survived into the 1950s. It is still operated as a tourist attraction at Orbisonia on US 522.

A portion of the Iron Horse Trail north of PA 274 has become impassable in places, but the southern part can still be hiked by using a car shuttle. Two trailheads are provided for this hike, both on PA 274. The western is on Hemlock Road next to Big Spring State Park, 4.8 miles northeast from the junction of PA 274 and PA 75 near Doylesburg. (This is the same trailhead as used in Hike 1 in this book.) Leave one car here. The eastern trailhead—from which you will begin—is 4.0 miles to the east, on the south side of PA 274 and just 0.8 mile west of the Tuscarora State Forest headquarters. Due to the rocky railroad grades you will want your hiking boots for this hike.

To start the hike, walk west along the highway for 600 meters, passing the Eby Cemetery on the north side of the highway; then turn left on a jeep road. John Eby and his brother-in-law, Peter Long, moved here in 1843 and introduced the German Baptists into this area. Services were held in a large house built on John Eby's farm, since most of the members' houses were too small. The Eby Cemetery

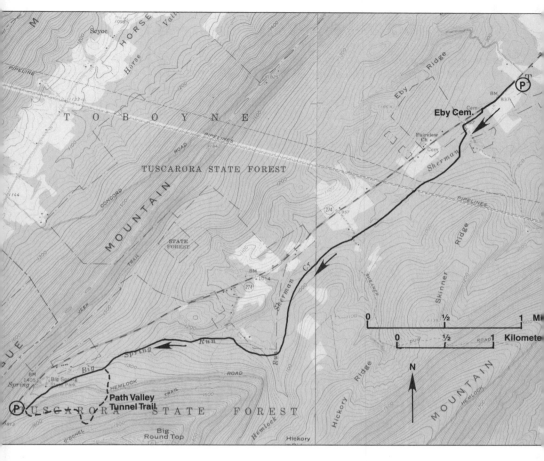

was the burial ground for the members.

Next, the red-blazed trail turns right through some Virginia pines. At 1 km you cross Sherman Creek on footbridges. Beyond the creek bear upstream; soon you pick up the Perry Lumber Company grade. Note parallel depressions caused by ties rotting in place. Only the steel was salvaged. At 1.7 km you cross a pair of pipelines, and then a footbridge over a run. Shortly the trail diverges from the grade and at 2.6 km you cross a gravel road. To the right this road crosses Sherman Creek and leads to PA 274.

To continue the hike, follow a woods road past a hunting camp. Soon it becomes evident you are on the old railroad grade again. At 3.6 km you bear left on another old grade and begin an extensive excursion around some private land. Cross Hemlock Run on a footbridge, then make a brief climb, still skirting the white-blazed private land boundary. Soon you turn downhill and cross Big Spring Run at 5.1 km. Turn left on the railroad grade and follow it upstream, crossing the run on bridges three more times.

The blue-blazed Path Valley Tunnel

Trail comes in from the left at 6.8 km. Continue through Big Spring State Park, passing a picnic shelter on the right and pit toilets on the left. At 7.4 km you reach the western trailhead and parking lot on Hemlock Road, where you left your other car.

Then drop in on the Tuscarora State Forest office and volunteer to help re-open the trail north of PA 274.

Additional hiking opportunities in this area include Hemlocks Natural Area (Hike 2) and Path Valley Railroad Tunnel (Hike 1). The orange-blazed Tuscarora Trail also traverses Tuscarora State Forest and can be reached from Hemlock Road just beyond Hemlocks Natural Area.

7

Little Buffalo State Park

Distance: 9.2 km (5.7 miles)

Time: 3¼ hours

Vertical Rise: 100 meters (330 ft)

Highlights: Covered bridge, bluebird trail

Maps: USGS 7.5' Newport; park map

One of the most delightful hikes in the state park system circles a recreational reservoir in Perry County. Attractions at Little Buffalo State Park in the Juniata Valley also include a covered bridge, a functioning water-powered gristmill, and a 25-post nature trail. There is a bluebird trail along the route. Alert hikers who see a bird smaller than a robin carrying the sky on its back will recognize the now rare bird loved by Thoreau and so many others. The bluebird trail consists of many birdhouses arranged along the route. Sparrows and starlings nest earlier than bluebirds so a park system volunteer must inspect the nesting boxes daily during nesting season and evict unwanted tenants. With luck and perseverance a

considerable colony of bluebirds may be established.

This hike's terrain is unusually varied, with thick woods on the south giving way to a stream bank and rolling meadows on the north. There are no strenuous climbs, but there is a fair amount of walking up and down hills. Walking shoes are probably adequate but a few rocky sections and some wet spots make hiking boots preferable. Watch out for poison ivy along the stream. Also, you may want to pick up the nature trail guide at the park office before you begin. The trail is yellow-blazed, in part, and is marked with signs at some intersections. It is usually well graded and easy to follow. The tags showing a dog walking on its hind legs with a cane were placed here by a volksmarch club. These tags do not necessarily mark the route of this hike.

To reach Little Buffalo State Park, drive south from US 322 at Newport on PA 34 for 2.9 miles to Little Buffalo Creek Road. Turn right, and then turn left on New Bloomfield Road, just after park headquarters. Follow the symbols for the hikers' parking lot, which also serves the gristmill.

Begin your hike by the signboard map at the far edge of the parking lot. Bear left on the gravel road between the

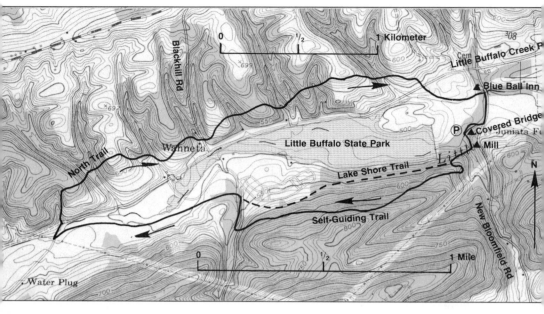

stream and the lot and then head right to Clay's Bridge. Originally this covered bridge spanned the creek 1.6 km west of this spot. It was moved here when the reservoir dam was built in the early 1970s, and now it carries only foot traffic. Just up the bank on the far side of the bridge you come to Shoaff's Mill, which grinds cornmeal on weekends. The overshot waterwheel was built on this site in 1832.

You now return to the railroad grade you crossed between the bridge and mill and turn left, upstream, on the bed of the old Newport and Sherman's Valley Railroad. The narrow-gauge line served this area from the early 1890s to 1929. (At the Path Valley Railroad Tunnel in Hike 1 you can see where the attempt to extend this railroad into the next valley came to grief.) Some 200 meters later the old railroad grade goes under the dam, and you turn left to the trail junction and left again onto the self-guiding trail, which makes a switchback up the hillside. This path leads 2.4 km through a young hemlock forest and past stump sprouts of native American chestnut, as well as oak and maple. The charcoal flats you see are reminders that a local iron industry flourished here in the Juniata Valley.

Follow the path to a junction in the picnic area, and turn left. (If you wish to return to your car at this point, turn right on the Lake Shore Trail for the 1.6-km walk back to the parking lot.) You are again following the grade of the N & SVRR. After a short walk you come to a meadow planted with thousands of pines and hybrid poplars, which will soon become woods.

You next take the mowed path to the right as it swings off the grade and moves along the south bank of Little Buffalo Creek. Walk quietly and you may surprise a bittern or little green heron, or even a great blue heron. The latter may surprise *you* when it flies off, for it is a sizable bird.

At the end of this stretch turn right on the paved Little Buffalo Creek Road, cross the bridge, and then turn off the road and

Functioning gristmill in Little Buffalo State Park

climb the bank. The North Trail now winds up through the woods and emerges at the edge of a meadow, where a bench permits rest and a view of the lake and wooded south side. The bluebird trail has been built along this stretch.

As you resume walking through these old fields, you at times descend to cross tiny brooks that flow to Little Buffalo Creek and at other times range into the woods farther up the slopes. At places the slopes are dry and Virginia pines flourish, but in the draws the water-loving hemlocks take over. You may notice a row of chestnut trees at one point beyond Blackhill Road. These are not American chestnuts, but oriental chestnuts planted

in the dooryard of a house now gone.

Suddenly the trail leaves the woods for the last time, crosses a field and Little Buffalo Creek Road again. It then parallels the overflow stream from the dam spillway until it reaches the Blue Ball Tavern. This tavern was the halfway house on the turnpike from Carlisle to Sunbury in the early 19th century and is now partly restored and open as a museum, thanks to the Perry County Historical Society.

To bring your hike to an end, turn right on the paved road, cross the creek again, and walk on the grass between the woods and road. Turn right on the next road, which takes you to the parking lot and your car.

8

Sideling Hill

Distance: 9.9 km (6.2 miles)

Time: 3¼ hours

Vertical Rise: 275 meters (900 ft)

Highlights: Mountain stream

Maps: USGS 7.5' Breezewood, Wells Tannery

Sideling Hill is unusually wide, thus permitting a circuit hike more or less on top of the ridge. The knife edges of Tuscarora, Tussey, and most other ridges do not permit this luxury. The hill's width made Sideling Hill Tunnel the longest of the nine tunnels on W.H. Vanderbilt's South Penn Railway. When work on "Vanderbilt's Folly" came to a halt in 1885, not one of the tunnels had been holed through, and the one at Sideling Hill was the farthest from completion. In the late 1930s Sideling Hill Tunnel was completed—for the Pennsylvania Turnpike instead of a railroad. By the 1960s the two-lane tunnel had become a bottleneck on a four-lane road, and along with the nearby Rays Hill Tunnel, it was by-passed when the turnpike was rerouted up and over both ridges.

No views exist along the trail itself, but the Cliff Trail leads to one at the eastern edge of Sideling Hill. The circuit hike is marked with blue blazes. You will probably want your hiking boots due to wet places, stream crossings, and rocks.

To reach the trail, drive east on US 30 from Breezewood 5.5 miles to Sideling Hill. Turn right on Bark Road at the east edge of Sideling Hill picnic area, drive 0.2 mile, and then bear right on Tower Road. You pass through a colonnade of red pines to reach the base of the fire tower. Park at the side to allow access to the buildings around the clearing. The fire tower has been fenced off and locked up, but the views were magnificent.

Begin by turning east onto the signed Cliff Trail. Following the trail, you'll soon move quickly out of the pine plantation and through a scrubby growth of chestnut oaks with many American chestnut sprouts. Cliff Trail soon starts its gentle descent to the stream.

About 500 meters farther, turn right onto Rock Oak Road. When the road forks, bear right on Rock Oak Road as the Cliff Trail goes straight ahead. To reach the view you would have to continue on the Cliff Trail to the edge of

Rock-hopping across Roaring Run

Sideling Hill and return the same way (this adds about 1.5 km to the hike).

A small stream drains into the East Fork of Roaring Run at 1.5 km; soon after, you enter a gypsy moth salvage cut made in 1994 along Rock Oak Road. All the trees cut were dead or dying from being defoliated by the caterpillars. A critical junction with the Roaring Run Trail is still marked with a sign reading "Rock Oak Road," but the actual trail has been buried under piles of slash. Slash consists of branches and treetops and is left on a logged area both to retard erosion and to promote regeneration of the forest. Without slash, a forest's new growth would be heavily browsed by deer; the deer are lazy, though, and don't push their way into slash. Continue on the Rock Oak Road for another 250 meters and then turn right on a logging road which soon swings left to follow the route of Roaring Run Trail. On your left there is an earlier clear-cut made in 1992. Notice the vigorous growth of saplings.

When the logging is completed, the slash will be pulled back from the trails, and the logging roads will be planted with orchard grass, clover, and bird's-foot trifoil and closed to vehicles. These grassy areas will also provide insects, and hen turkeys and grouse will bring their broods here as soon as they are out of the nest. So keep your eyes open. Be careful not to step on any of the chicks.

Jackson Trail joins Roaring Run Trail for a bit; bear right on it where the logging road goes left. Soon Jackson Trail turns right. (The hike can be truncated by turning right on Jackson Trail and then right again on Bald Hill Trail.) Just before Jackson cuts off, a spring turns the trail muddy for a distance. As you reach the East Fork of Roaring Run the trail tunnels through a dense growth of rhododendron and hemlock. You cross the stream on stepping-stones at 4 km and again at 4.6 km. Now the trail becomes rockier.

You shortly come upon the unsigned Peck Trail, and at 5.5 km you turn right on a jeep road and then cross the run on a snowmobile bridge. A short way beyond, turn right, *uphill*, on the signed Bald Hill Trail. From here, you have nowhere to go but up. At rocky places the footway may vanish, but the way is straight and you shouldn't have any trouble picking it up again.

At 6.3 km you recross Peck Trail; this time both trails are signed, as are the junctions with Jackson Trail at 7.6 km and Deer Hill Trail at 8.1 km. Soon you cross an unsigned trail, and at 9.8 km you reach a gravel road leading to one of the several microwave antennas on Bald Knob. From here it is a short distance to the fire tower and your car.

9

Old Loggers Trail

Distance: 9.9 km (6.2 miles)	

Time: 3¼ hours

Vertical Rise: 350 meters (1140 ft)

Highlights: View

Maps: USGS 7.5' Huntingdon; Old Loggers Trail Map

The Old Loggers Trail in Huntingdon County is not to be confused with the much longer Old Loggers Path in Lycoming County. The Old Loggers Trail is on Corps of Engineers land surrounding Raystown Lake. Like most of Pennsylvania, these lands have been logged repeatedly. The trail follows old farm roads, logging roads, and game trails.

The Old Loggers Trail is located 3.6 miles from PA 26 on the access road to the Seven Points campground. There is no need to stop at the contact station. There is a small parking area on your right just across from the trailhead. Walking shoes are adequate for this hike.

To start the hike, cross the road and pass the map board. Note the Sheep Rock Spur, which provides a view of Raystown Lake. The blue-blazed trail climbs gently and then descends into a stream valley, passing the ruins of a springhouse. The spring has dried up.

After a couple of stream crossings the trail reaches an inlet of Raystown Lake and bears left above the water's edge. Cross a larger stream and you reach a trail junction at 2.0 km. Turn left and climb gently along an old woods road paralleling the stream. At 3.5 km turn right and continue climbing. At the edge of the road to the Susquehanna Campground, turn right again. This spot would serve as an alternative access point, except that out of season the road is gated off.

In just 200 meters turn left on the Sheep Rock Spur at an unsigned junction. Sheep Rock was a natural shelter along the Raystown Branch of the Juniata River. Salvage archaeology conducted by Pennsylvania State University in the early 1960s showed that this site was used at least 8000 years ago. It is now submerged 30 meters beneath the waters of Raystown Lake.

After 500 meters turn right at a trail sign to an overlook far above the lake. Below you can see Marti's Island and, in the distance, Seven Points Recreation Area, Marina, and Campground, with Terrace Mountain stretching off to the south.

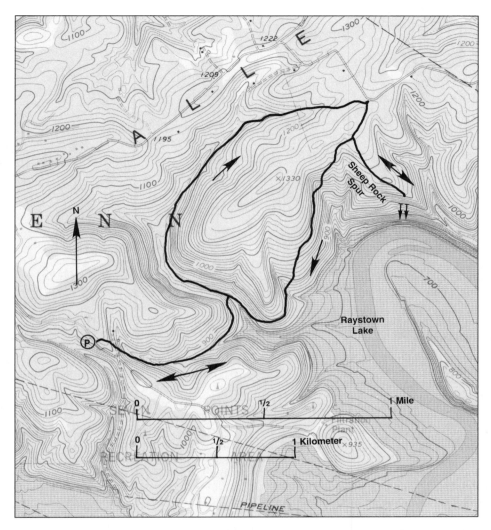

There are only a few views of the lake of this quality, and this may well be the best. Then retrace your steps on the Sheep Rock Spur and turn left on the main trail. The trail becomes narrow and descends to an old road where you turn right.

The old road soon dives into the lake but you bear right on a new trail to where another road emerges from the lake.

Bear right on this road to the main trail junction. Turn left here and retrace your steps to your car.

Other hiking opportunities at Raystown Lake include the Terrace Mountain Trail on the east side of the lake, and the trail system at Trough Creek State Park (Hike 11), also on the east side of the lake.

10

Flat Rock

Distance: 11.2 km (7.0 miles)	
Time: 4 hours	
Vertical Rise: 503 meters (1650 ft)	
Highlights: View	
Maps: USGS 7.5' Andersonburg; park trail map	

Natural overlooks are rare in Pennsylvania and trails to them are rarer still. From Flat Rock you are treated to a spectacular view across the Cumberland Valley from one such overlook on the crest of Blue Mountain. This hike is located in Colonel Denning State Park, named for a hero of the American Revolution. The hike traverses the park's length and offers several optional routes as you return from the natural overlook area. The park is on PA 233 in a valley formed by a hairpin bend of Blue Mountain. To reach it drive 3.4 miles north from the junction with PA 997 at McCrea, or 7.9 miles southwest from the junction with PA 850 at Landisburg. Wear your hiking boots for this rocky trail.

You begin the Flat Rock Trail at the nature center parking area, which is on the road to the camping area. Cross Doubling Gap Creek on a footbridge (the hike's red blazes begin here), climb the steps beyond, and then continue on fairly level ground for the next 600 meters. Now turn left on a jeep road and start a serious climb. After some 200 meters you pass a springhouse; bear right and climb easily for a bit. A final pitch of steep climbing brings you to a major trail junction, the Wagon Wheel, or Hub, atop Blue Mountain. You have traveled a total of 1.7 km.

For obscure reasons the Tuscarora Trail, which is usually blazed orange, is instead blazed pink at the Wagon Wheel! Maintenance of the Tuscarora has been taken over by the Potomac Appalachian Trail Club, so the orange blazes could be reinstated at any time. The Woodburn Trail comes in about 60 meters to your right. The Lehman Trail is on your left, and the red-blazed Warner Trail is on your extreme left. At the turn of the century a barrel stave mill operated somewhere near this point. The staves were carried down the mountain by horse and wagon on what is now the Tuscarora Trail.

Continue on Flat Rock Trail—which is also the Tuscarora—across the Wagon

1 Mile

½

1 Kilometer

½

N

Cider Path

Spring

Doub

CUMP

1687

1661

LOWER

150

P

STATE PARK

CROCE BENING

1600

950

1100

1350

1650

1450

1300

MIFFLIN

FOREST

Trout

Warner Trail

Creek

TENNING
ATE PARK BM

750

Ridge

1600

Tuscarora Trail

Flat Rock

1794

Buck

×1732

T Y

1888 ×

Woodburn

Trail

Trail

TUSCARORA

Lehman
Trail

Wildcat Ridge

WILD

165

1350

1450

Tuscarora
Trail

1600

1943

PERRY COUNTY

CUMBERLAND COUNTY

1987   Flat Rock

UPPER   FL

1138

Cumberland Valley from Flat Rock

Wheel, following red blazes and pink blazes. The trail dips gently into Wildcat Hollow and crosses an intermittent run. You then climb to the top of Blue Mountain and, just over the crest, come upon Flat Rock, which has one of the best views in the state. On a clear day you see across the Cumberland Valley to heavily wooded South Mountain. This is the great valley of the Appalachians, extending some 3000 km from northern Georgia to Montreal. Be mindful of the dropoff at the edge of Flat Rock. The Tuscarora diverges to the east from Flat Rock and one return option is to follow it into Wildcat Hollow where it joins the Lehman Trail. You would then turn left on the Lehman Trail to return to the Wagon Wheel.

You can also simply retrace your steps 1.6 km on Flat Rock Trail to the Wagon Wheel. You could shorten the hike at this point by continuing straight down the Flat Rock Trail, or taking either the Tuscarora or Woodburn Trails, now at your left. These lead to PA 233, and you would walk along the highway back to the park.

Your final option, and the one described here, is to bear right on the Warner Trail, which slabs the end of Buck Ridge. You cross over Blue Mountain and continue to a log landing, where you encounter a recent logging road. Follow the logging road for several hundred meters to where the Warner Trail diverges to the right. Then continue on the Warner, crossing a stream and climbing to the top of Lays Ridge. Here you intersect Cider Path. Turn left on this red-blazed trail for a gentle climb to the top of Blue Mountain, rejoining the logging road at the top. Take a sharp left turn on a trail at the top of the ridge and walk 50 meters of a rocky footway before joining an old log skid. Such log skids were used to move logs down the mountain. The Cider Path follows the log skid down the ridge, becoming a woods road before it intersects the Doubling Gap Road toward the bottom of the valley. Turn left on Doubling Gap Road for about 200 meters to the park boundary.

Continue along Doubling Gap Road, bearing right at two junctions to reach the beach. Toward the beach area's far end bear right and cross the creek on the road bridge. Then bear left through the beach parking area. At the far right corner find the end of a Youth Conservation Corps nature trail that takes you back to the nature center and your car.

11

Trough Creek State Park

Distance: 11.9 km (7.4 miles)

Time: 5 hours

Vertical Rise: 480 meters (1575 ft)

Highlights: Ice mine, balanced rock, waterfalls, views

Maps: USGS 7.5' Cassville, Entriken; park map

Hikers visiting this Huntingdon County site will be treated to a mammoth sandstone boulder balanced on the edge of Trough Creek Gorge and an ice mine that produces ice well into the summer. The boulder is termed an "erosion remnant" and probably has not moved very far from where it broke off a rock cliff that has since weathered away. At Copperas Rock, which is also on this hike, you see what may be an earlier stage in this process.

The ice mine is simply a hole in the ground that lies at the base of a slope covered with a thick layer of broken rock. During the winter, cold air is drawn in at the base of the slope and cools the rock

as it rises. In late spring, this flow reverses. The cold rocks then chill the air that finally emerges at the base of the slope. In the mine the cold air comes into contact with moist air from the outside and freezes the vapor on the rocks.

Although this is an enjoyable hike anytime, the falls along the way are most spirited in the high water of spring and early summer or after heavy rains. Due to its length and many wet spots you will appreciate your boots on this hike.

To reach the site turn east onto PA 994 from PA 26 between Shy Beaver and Marklesburg. Drive through the village of Entriken, across Raystown Lake, and after 5.3 miles turn north at the sign for Trough Creek State Park. After 1.8 miles bear left on Trough Creek Drive for just 0.2 mile to a parking lot on the right with a map board. Park here.

To begin your hike cross the road and head up the blue-blazed Ledges Trail. Keep right at the top of the ledge. Pass the ruins of a cabin on your left and several views on your right. Round Mountain can be seen to the south. Turn right on the Copperas Rock Trail at 1.1 km and descend along a ridgeline through a stand of hemlocks. Near the bottom the Rhododendron Trail comes in on your left. (One way to truncate this hike would

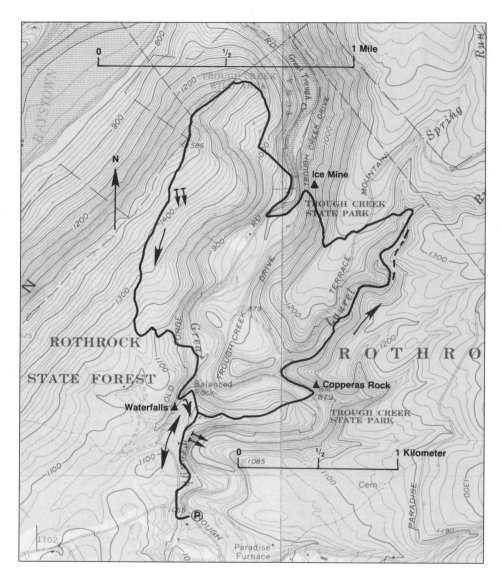

be to turn left on this trail and follow it to the Abbot Run Trail, where you would again turn left.) Continue on the Copperas Rock Trail for another 100 meters, then turn left on Trough Creek Drive. Copperas Rock overhangs the creek beyond the picnic area.

Take the bridge over the creek, swing left through another picnic area, and just beyond the parking lot turn right on the green-blazed Laurel Run Trail. After crossing Laurel Run six times you reach a junction with an old road from the right called the Loop Trail, which re-

Footbridge over Trough Creek

turns to the Laurel Run Trail after two more crossings. Continue upstream past this junction, crossing the run again, and then switchback up the side of the valley. You soon jog left across Terrace Mountain Road.

About 600 meters farther you bear right at a trail junction and soon begin the descent into Trough Creek on the red-blazed Ice Mine Trail. It leads gently downhill toward the ice mine, which stays quite cold through August, long after it has stopped producing ice. After inspecting the mine, turn left on the paved road and then right to a parking lot. Pass a large signboard at the corner of the parking lot and cross the footbridge over Trough Creek. Climb the bank and turn right on Old Forge Road, which is also the blue-blazed Terrace Mountain Trail. (Your last opportunity to truncate this hike is to turn left on the Old Forge Road and follow it to a hunting camp, where you would turn left.)

After about 300 meters turn left on the orange-blazed Brumbaugh Trail. Climb steeply on a logging road and then continue along the corner of the ridge. With the leaves down there is an extensive view of Raystown Lake from this ridge.

The trail follows the ridgeline up a final pitch to the top of Terrace Mountain. White blazes visible to the right mark the boundary of Rothrock State Forest. The trail still becomes obscure at the top of the ridge. Cross over the ridgeline and continue parallel to it on the far side. Gypsy moths have killed many trees at this point, letting in the sunlight, which has produced a dense growth of striped maple. Soon the trail is back among live trees and blazes become more frequent. The Brumbaugh then picks up an old charcoal road, as evidenced by slag in the footway.

Next you pass a series of salvage cuts resulting in part from a forest fire here in

November 1991. The fire doesn't seem to have been too destructive above ground, but it burned deeply into the soil and was difficult to put out. Evidently this killed a lot of trees. You can see Round and Buinns Mountains to the south, and Shirley Knob, with its microwave towers, to the east. Pass a log landing from an earlier timber sale. Next, a couple of woods roads come in from your right. Blazes become scarce as the trail switchbacks downhill to the Old Forge Road.

Continue across this road and bear right on an unmarked trail. After about 100 meters turn right on the yellow-blazed Raven Rock Trail. This takes you to Balanced Rock and a good view of the valley. Then follow the white-blazed Abbot Run Trail down into Abbot Run, passing a junction with the Rhododendron Trail. (The largest waterfall on Abbot Run is to your left on the Rhododendron Trail.) Back on the Abbot Run Trail, proceed upstream, crossing a bridge over the run. After another 100 meters turn left on the Ledges Trail and climb past a view. At 10.9 km you pass the junction with the Copperas Rock Trail and retrace your steps to your car, remembering to bear left at the utility line.

Other hiking opportunities at Raystown Lake include the Terrace Mountain Trail, on this side of the lake, and the Old Loggers Trail (Hike 9) on the road to Seven Points Recreation Area, on the other side.

12

Blue Knob State Park

Distance: 16.3 km (10.1 miles)

Time: 6¼ hours

Vertical Rise: 500 meters (1640 ft)

Highlights: Mountain streams

Maps: USGS 7.5' Blue Knob; Lost Turkey Trail

Blue Knob State Park protects the second highest point in the state and is one of five demonstration parks operated in Pennsylvania by the National Park Service in the 1930s. A rather elaborate trail system was built in the park then. After World War II these parks were turned over to the Commonwealth of Pennsylvania. Over the years, many of the old trails were abandoned while others were downgraded into roads. In the late 1970s several of the remaining trails were incorporated into a new, long-distance hiking trail that linked Blue Knob State Park with Babcock Picnic Area on PA 56. This new trail was named the Lost Turkey Trail by the Youth Conservation Corps who blazed it in 1976, and the story behind the name shall remain untold to save embarrassment to the two experienced woodspersons who scouted the route.

This hike, which covers the best of the Lost Turkey Trail, is on state park, private, and state game land. The Lost Turkey name does not appear on any trail signs but the trail was provided with kilometer posts, many of which remain. However, the Lost Turkey was not the first metric hiking trail in the United States. The Mid State Trail was metricated at least 3 years earlier. My measurements with a 2-meter measuring wheel show an unresolved discrepancy with the kilometer posts. For a free map of the Lost Turkey Trail (and adjoining John P. Saylor Trail, Hike 14) write to: Blue Knob State Park, RD 1, Imler, PA 16655.

Blue Knob State Park is 20 miles north of Bedford and the Pennsylvania Turnpike via US 220 and PA 869. If you approach from the north, exit US 220 at King but turn north to Sproul. Turn west and drive through Queen to Pavia. This hike requires a car shuttle. One end is at the Burnt House Picnic Area on PA 869, 2.0 miles west of Pavia. Leave one car here and drive back to Pavia. Turn left on Forrest Road for 3.7 miles, passing the park office and family campground. Turn right on the road to the ski area for

0.6 mile and then park along the road as best you can where the paved but gated side road leads to Herman Point. Hiking boots are in order for this hike.

To start your hike, head up the road to Herman Point. There are several radio antennas in a clearing at the top but the fire tower has been dismantled. The red-blazed Lost Turkey Trail starts behind the unfenced white-painted block building. The trail leads into the woods and soon starts down the western flank of Herman Point, passing an old overlook long since shut in by resurgent trees. At the top you descend on stone steps.

At 1.5 km jog left across the paved road, very close to the corner of the ski area road. Occasionally you see the number 11 painted on trees or rocks, indicating that this was Trail No. 11 from the park's original trail system. Shortly you stop descending and bear left on an old grade.

At 2.2 km you cross the white-blazed boundary of State Game Lands 26. According to the map you are some distance up the hill from this boundary. After passing km post 2, you come to a corner of the family campground. This is the highest campground anywhere in the Pennsylvania state park system and has never been full—even on the 4th of July weekend. The trail skirts the edge of the campground but at one point passes right through several campsites. In the second of these campsites, it makes an obscure right-angle turn to the right and proceeds down Conrad Ridge on old Trail No. 10. After passing km post 3, the descent becomes steep.

At 4.7 km you reach the bottom and turn right on the road up Rhodes Run. There are several surplus double blazes along this road before you reach a left turn marked with an arrow. Bear left onto trail-crossing footbridges over Rhodes and Ciana Runs.

At 5.4 km you reach the memorial to the Lost Cox Children of the Alleghenies, whose bodies were found here in 1856. The two Cox boys, aged 5 and 7, wandered away from home and were found dead here about 2 weeks later. The finder, a neighbor of the Coxes, said the location of the bodies had appeared to him in a recurrent dream. Today the finder would probably be charged with murder. People were more credulous in the 19th century, as well as superstitious.

The trail continues up Ciana Run, crossing it repeatedly. For the most part, the trail follows an old logging railroad grade of the Babcock Lumber Company. The railroad logging of this part of Penn's Woods was delayed by the old Pennsylvania Canal Dam on the South Fork of the Conemaugh River. The dam outlived the canal and became a rustic retreat. This was the dam that burst on May 31, 1889, producing the Johnstown Flood. The optimal railroad route to this part of the forest led up the South Fork of the Conemaugh. Within a year of the flood, a railroad had been laid through the gap, and the cutting of the virgin forests was underway.

At 7.0 km, when you reach the forks of Ciana Run, turn sharp left; the trail has become very obscure from here to the power line. After crossing the power-line swath you pick up the trail again. Next you climb to the top of Hog Back Ridge at 7.7 km. At the top jog left on a jeep road for about 100 meters. On the far side of the ridge the trail swings south and descends on a well-graded footway. At the bank of Bobs Creek, 8.5 km, you turn left, downstream. Shortly the trail crosses Bobs Creek on a cable bridge. Put your feet on the lower cable and hold onto the upper one, then move across the creek sideways.

Once on the far side, the trail heads inland, crosses a railroad grade, and then heads downstream on the slope beyond, thus avoiding a section of the grade that has been washed out. At 9.0 km, you pick up the railroad grade again and follow it past km post 8 to a right turn at 9.4 km, which is marked by a small sign saying "Bobs Creek." The trail soon picks up another railroad grade, which follows Ickes Run. After passing km post 9, you cross Ickes Run, the last water until you reach Burnt House Picnic Area.

Soon you cross the now dry streambed and shortly turn sharp left across the streambed for a last time. This crossing and turn were obscured by blowdowns on my hike. The trail now proceeds east, still climbing. After another left turn, the trail slabs the hillside without benefit of side hill construction but with occasional views of Herman Point and Blue Knob through grapevine tangles.

The trail has trouble holding its elevation and there are a lot of ups and downs. The motivation behind this protracted traverse may have been to avoid some private land on the top of Forks Ridge. Near 11.8 km the trail appears to top out but this is premature; it soon drops off the edge of the ridge again.

At 12.7 km new white blazes herald a recent addition to State Game Lands 26. Soon you bear left on a woods road but at last you are firmly on top of Forks Ridge. Kilometer post 12 is passed as you bear left on another woods road. By now, the 7.5 percent discrepancy between the posts and my measurements, compounded by the measurements starting at the road rather than the top of Herman Point, is becoming confusing. The trail continues down Forks Ridge on these delightful woods roads, crossing private and park lands and an-

Spring at Burnt House Picnic Area

other section of state game land. The private land just beyond has been recently logged, destroying the trail. If the trail has not been reopened turn right along the game land boundary and then left along the park boundary, skirting the piles of slash.

Pick up the Lost Turkey Trail in a ravine where it descends the west side of Forks Ridge. Turn right onto the trail and descend through this ravine to Wallacks Branch. Cross as best you can. The trail is overgrown and hard to follow beyond the stream, but you soon strike an old road grade. Bear left and it will bring you out to PA 869. Cross the highway and bear left through the Burnt House Picnic Area. There is a piped spring just to the right of the picnic shelter, and the parking lot where you left your car is across the footbridge to your left.

Additional hiking opportunities in Blue Knob State Park can be found on other fragments of the old trail system; the Lost Turkey Trail, too, continues up Big Break Hollow. There are nearby hikes at the Allegheny Portage Railroad (Hike 4) and on the John P. Saylor Trail (Hike 14) on PA 56 near Windber.

13

Lower Trail

Distance: 17.8 km (11.1 miles)

Time: 5½ hours

Vertical Rise: none

Highlights: Pennsylvania canal; iron furnace

Maps: USGS 7.5' Spruce Creek, Williamsburg; Lower Trail

The Lower Trail (pronounced Laurer) is a new trail along the Frankstown Branch of the Juniata River from Alfarata in Huntingdon County to Williamsburg in Blair County. The trail follows the grade of the Pennsylvania Railroad, which was abandoned in 1982. The railroad in turn followed the route of the Pennsylvania Canal. The Frankstown Indian Path cut across country for the most part along the route followed by US 22 today. The Frankstown Path was named for Frank Stevens, who had a trading post at a Native American village near Hollidaysburg.

The Penns Creek Path joined the Frankstown Path at Water Street. Water Street was so named because pack trains bound for trading posts farther west used the riverbed through the narrow gap in Tussey Ridge.

Abandoned railroads do not automatically become trails. Most of them are lost when adjacent landowners convert them to their own purposes. Rails-to-Trails of Blair County, Inc., PO Box 592, Hollidaysburg, PA 16648, purchased the entire Petersburg Branch from the Penn Central Corporation in March 1991. The purchase was made possible by a generous donation from T. Dean Lower, a local attorney, in memory of his wife, Jane Lower, and son, Raymond D. Lower.

Etna Furnace, a charcoal iron furnace dating back to 1807, is just a few hundred meters west of the Lower Trail. Etna Furnace is scheduled to become a national historic site. Ironically, aluminum I-beams have been used to stabilize the stack.

The northern end of this car shuttle hike is at the new trailhead in Alfarata. You can reach Alfarata from US 22 by taking Alexandria Road (SR 4014) just west of the highway bridge over the Frankstown Branch of the Juniata River. The parking lot is 0.2 mile from US 22 at the old railroad crossing. Park one car here. Drive your other car back to US 22 and turn right. Drive west for 6.5 miles, then turn left on the road to Williamsburg

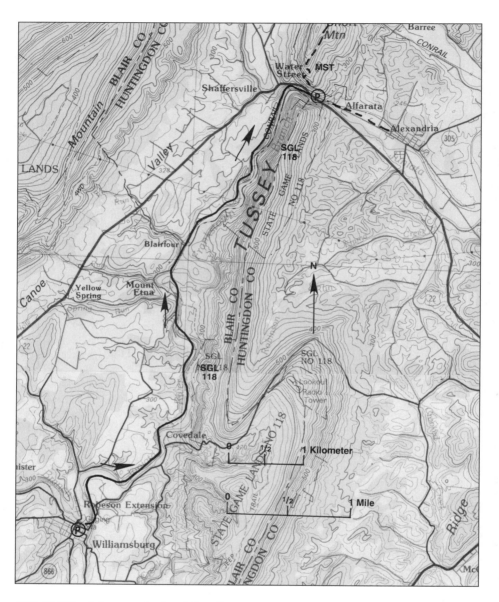

(SR 2015); drive south for 4.5 miles. Take the first left after the bridge (First Street) and park at the Williamsburg trailhead on your left. Despite its length this hike is on good footway so walking shoes should be fine.

Walk up to the old railroad grade and bear right. The Lower Trail is a multiple-use trail with grade separation. Hikers get a 4-foot-wide strip planted with grass on the right side. Bikers get an 8-foot-wide strip in the middle, paved with crushed

Author at southern trailhead of Lower Trail

limestone, while horses have a 5-foot grassy swath on the far side. There is a 2-foot separation between these different grades. Now all that is required is for each group to stay on its own grade.

At 800 meters you reach the ruins of the lockhouse for Lock 67. Only below-ground remnants remain. Mileposts from the railroad era remain but newer wooden posts giving the distance in both directions have also been installed. At 1.6 km the trail detours around a field. You reach the first bridge over the Franks-town Branch at 2.7 km, and the ruins of Lockhouse 64 at 3.0 km. Little remains. Moving on, you pass some low cliffs to your left and then a large power line overhead. At 5.2 km you reach an inter-mediate trailhead and parking lot. The Lower Trail continues through bottom-lands along the Frankstown Branch to another access point at 9.4 km. Soon you reach the second bridge over the river, followed shortly by the third and final

bridge. All these bridges have been decked and provided with railings.

Just beyond the last bridge is another access point—this one from T 482. The Lower Trail passes through a cut and then skirts a large pond on private land. Fox Run, which forms the boundary be-tween Blair and Huntingdon Counties, is crossed on a stone culvert. The river is again visible to your right.

At 12.3 km the trail enters a canyon with limestone cliffs on your left and the steep side of Tussey Mountain across the river. Listen for the call of the pileated woodpecker. State Game Land (SGL) 118 is on the far side of the river. From here on the trail has a wilder aspect.

Next you pass under a high-voltage transmission line that jumps to the top of Tussey Mountain in a single bound. This side of Tussey was extensively quarried for a sandstone called ganister. Origi-nally used for lining iron furnaces, such as Mount Etna, it was later used for fill along the railroad. In the winter when snow conditions are just right, several quarry levels can be seen on the flank of Tussey. You pass the ruins of the Goodman Quarry on your left at 13.6 km.

Limestone from the Goodman and Owens Quarries was probably used as flux at iron furnaces. Just beyond the Goodman Quarry are what appear to be abutments for a bridge across the Frankstown Branch. This bridge led to a cable railway or funicular that served the quarry levels on the side of Tussey Mountain. When snow conditions are just right, you can see the course of the funicular up the mountainside.

At 15.1 km you reach a remnant of the old Pennsylvania Canal that was not destroyed by the railroad. It certainly was of modest proportions. Beyond at the Owens Quarry, limestone again, there is a trail register. Please register so that Rails-to-Trails of Blair County can determine the usage level of the Lower Trail. After the peace and quiet of the Lower Trail, the roar of traffic on US 22 is a shock, but soon you pass behind the Water Street flea market. Continue on the railroad grade, which now parallels US 22, then pass under the highway to reach the Alfarata trailhead and your car.

Other hiking opportunities in the area include the southern end of the Mid State Trail (MST). This is about 0.2 mile west of the Alfarata trailhead at the junction of US 22 and Alexandria Road.

14

John P. Saylor Trail

Distance: 19.8 km (12.3 miles)

Time: 6½ hours

Vertical Rise: 120 meters (400 ft)

Highlights: Clear Shade Wild Area

Maps: USGS 7.5' Ogletown, Windber; John P. Saylor Trail

John P. Saylor became one of the great conservationists of our time during the 24 years he served in the US Congress. From 1949 until his death in 1973 he represented Pennsylvania's 22nd District, and for many years he was the senior Republican on the House Interior Committee. Among his accomplishments are sponsorship of the National Wilderness Preservation system and the National Scenic Trails Act. We are all in his debt.

As a memorial to Saylor a hiking trail has been blazed in Gallitzin State Forest in Somerset County. While the hike is long, traveling is easy since this region is on the Allegheny Plateau and much of the trail follows old roads and railroad grades. The only rough section is in the vicinity of Wolf Rocks near the trail's end. Nearly half the route traverses the 1129-hectare Clear Shade Wild Area.

Orange rectangles are used as markers, and mileposts have been installed along the trail. Blue blazes are posted on parts of the trail, but these mark the Babcock Ski Touring Trail. If you wish to camp overnight along the trail, obtain a permit from the district forest office in Ebensburg at 814-472-8320. You will want your hiking boots for this long hike.

The hike begins in the Babcock Picnic Area on PA 56 between Ogletown and Windber, where there is ample parking. Starting at the large sign, turn left and follow the trail along the edge of the picnic area. Fill your canteen as you pass the water pump. The trail bears right on old PA 56, which was the original wagon road between Bedford and Johnstown. Before that it was the Conemaugh Indian Path.

About 1.0 km from the start you cross the paved road to Ashtola. After this, the old road is gated and walking becomes more enjoyable. At 3.2 km you cross Shade Road and enter the Clear Shade Wild Area. As with most road crossings on this trail, it is gated to prevent vehicular traffic. After another 600 meters turn right onto a grassed-over timber haul road, where selective cutting operations

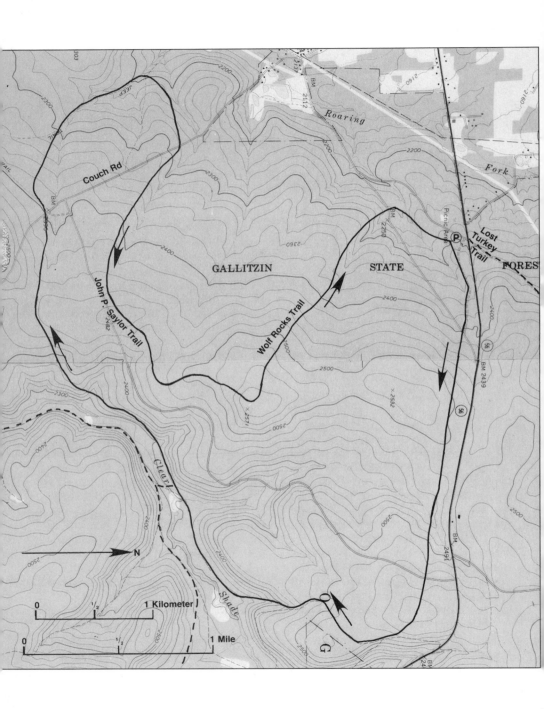

Roaring

Fork

Couch Rd

GALLITZIN   STATE   Lost
                                  Turkey
                                  Trail
                                  FORES

John P. Saylor Trail

Wolf Rocks Trail

Picnic Area

BM 2439

BM 2494

Clear

Shade

N

| 0 | ½ | 1 Kilometer |

| 0 | ½ | 1 Mile |

G

were conducted in 1962 and 1963 before the wild area was established. The old haul road is again easy walking.

After 2 km you turn right again, enter a band of extensive meadows along Clear Shade Creek, and then pick up an old logging railroad grade used by the Babcock Lumber Company around the turn of the century. You can tell you are on an old railroad grade by the occasional small fills and cuts required to keep the grade constant for steam locomotives. The meadows are the result of soil erosion, old forest fires, and probably a high water table along the nearby creek. These meadows and their woodland boundaries provide a diversity of wildlife habitats.

Some distance along you cross a large stream on a log bridge. Listen for the sound of water falling over the ruins of a splash dam on Clear Shade Creek. The splash dam was built in the last century to float logs down this stream, which otherwise would have been too shallow for a log drive, even during the spring runoff.

Near here an orange-blazed side trail goes left, crossing Clear Shade Creek on a footbridge to another loop of the John P. Saylor Trail south of the creek; this loop is not described in this hike.

Just past 8 km you bear right off the old railroad grade, bypass a wet spot once bridged by a high trestle, and start the climb out of the Clear Shade watershed. You soon rejoin the old railroad grade, which now climbs gently toward the plateau. This is the halfway point of the trail. After passing through more meadows, you cross Couch Road.

Immediately after crossing this road, the Saylor Trail bears right on another railroad grade down into a hollow toward Sandy Run. After crossing three different watercourses, which are probably intermittent this far up, you turn right, leaving the railroad grade for good, and soon pick up an old woods road that winds gently upward to Couch Road again.

After you recross Couch Road you hit the first lengthy section of real trail, which continues climbing gently past a recently logged area to the edge of a meadow. A slab-sided shelter has been built here but it does not appear attractive for camping. Turn left through the meadow, past the site of Logging Camp 59, which was used by the Babcock Lumber Company around 1900.

At the meadow's end you bear right and wind through the woods on the John P. Saylor Trail. The way becomes rougher and rockier and finally picks up the well-worn Wolf Rocks Trail (part of the John P. Saylor Trail). Once extensive views may have been available from the top of these rocks, but the trees have grown high and the views are disappointing. The Wolf Rocks site is still an eloquent argument for banning spray paint. These are the most vandalized rocks I have ever seen.

You now descend the rough trail past a spring at the base of Wolf Rocks, and after 1 km follow the trail under a pole line and jog right across a paved road. You cross two more streams before returning to the picnic area and your car. For a copy of the John P. Saylor Trail map, write to Gallitzin State Forest, 131 Hillcrest Drive, Ebensburg, PA 15931.

Other hiking opportunities near the John P. Saylor Trail can be found on the Lost Turkey Trail (Hike 12) and on other trails at Blue Knob State Park.

MIDDLE DISTRICT

15

Alan Seeger Trail

Distance: 2.0 km (1.2 miles)

Time: 30 minutes

Vertical Rise: None

Highlights: Virgin timber, rhododendrons

Maps: USGS 7.5' McAlevys Fort; MSTA map 203

In the Seven Mountains region of central Pennsylvania grows a small stand of old hemlocks known as the Alan Seeger Natural Area. In 1921, Colonel Henry Shoemaker, then a member of the Pennsylvania State Forest Commission, chose to name this area for a young American poet who was killed in France in World War I. According to a biography, Alan Seeger never ventured any closer to Pennsylvania than Staten Island. Curiously, though, a state forest map of the Seven Mountains dated February 1920 shows several sites with variations of the Seeger name, all of them to the north and west of the natural area. The poet's relationship to these places is unknown,

as is Shoemaker's reason for the commemoration.

This is an ideal first hike for children. Even 2-year-olds can hike it, and they delight in walking in the rhododendron tunnel, looking for fish in the streams, and getting their feet wet if they decide not to use the footbridges.

You reach the Alan Seeger Natural Area by driving west on the mostly paved Stone Creek Road 7.3 miles from US 322 at Laurel Creek Reservoir, or by traveling 6.4 miles east from PA 26 at McAlevys Fort. Walking shoes are fine for this short hike on good footway.

You begin walking the trail at the sign in the parking area next to the junction of Stone Creek and Seeger Roads. Another sign says the trail takes only 15 minutes to walk, but it's worth your while to take longer. The trail first winds through open woods. Many of the trees and shrubs along the way are identified by signs, which makes this an ideal walk for those who are still learning which is which. Among them are black birch, white oak, pitch pine, flowering dogwood, and red maple.

In about 450 meters the path intersects the Greenwood Spur of the Mid State Trail System. If you turn left and walk a short distance down the spur and

Alan Seeger Trail lined with rhododendron

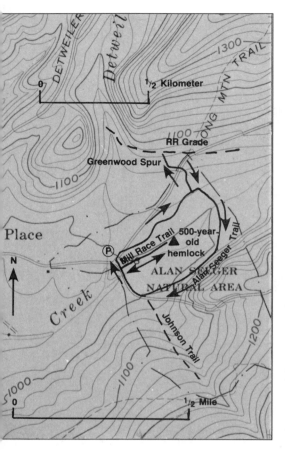

Retrace your steps to the junction, continue straight on the Alan Seeger Trail, and head toward the rhododendrons. In places these hardy bushes are 6 meters high and arch over the trail, creating a green tunnel. They are usually in full bloom the first week of July, making that an ideal time to hike this route. Off the trail, the jungle of rhododendrons is fully as impenetrable as it looks.

About halfway around the loop you come on some of the oldest trees in the state. Secure on their island in Stone Creek, they must have survived the summer of 1644, when most of Pennsylvania is believed to have burned over. Nobody knows just how old these trees really are, but they are considerably larger than the 500-year-old hemlock lying across the Mill Race Trail farther along this hike. Age estimates are based on their size with respect to other hemlocks in the same area that have been dated by ring counting. Since they are over twice the diameter of the Mill Race tree, 600 years is a very conservative estimate. The full extrapolation is 1200 years, and that's the best number we'll have until these trees die or fall over. (One tree fell over recently but was hollow, so we still don't have a firm estimate of its age.) Nobody is going to risk damaging them by taking a core sample. If they really are 1200 years old, they would rival the box huckleberry in Perry County as the oldest living things in Penn's Woods. Presumably most of the hemlocks in the Seven Mountains are descended from these specimens.

After crossing a footbridge over Stone Creek you bear right again through open woods. Shortly you arrive at Seeger Road, where the Greenwood Spur turns to the left, up Johnson Trail. Bear right on the road, following it back across Stone Creek to Mill Race Trail, where a right turn brings you to the 500-year-old hem-

across Stone Creek Road you encounter one of the mysteries of this area: the grade of a narrow-gauge railroad. The grade is the remnant of a logging railroad that led to Milroy and was used by several lumber companies around the turn of the century. The mystery lies in how the big trees in this area were spared in the logging operations, and even earlier in the widespread charcoal operation from Greenwood Iron Furnace on the far side of Broad Mountain. Charcoal flats can be found far up Grass Mountain beyond Alan Seeger. Why was this area bypassed?

lock, dated by actual ring counting. The millrace from which this trail takes its name carried water to a water-powered sawmill believed to have been called Milligan Mills. So, with the charcoal operations and a sawmill on one side and a logging railroad on another, the survival of this area's hemlocks becomes even more of a mystery.

You now retrace your steps to the road. A short distance to your right is the parking area, where there are picnic tables.

16

Snyder Middleswarth State Park

Distance: 5.4 km (3.4 miles)

Time: 2 hours

Vertical Rise: 230 meters (760 ft)

Highlights: Virgin timber

Map: USGS 7.5' Weikert

An extensive stand of old-growth timber along Swift Run in Bald Eagle State Forest is the setting for this hike. There are three tracts of land here. The smallest is the 3-hectare state park, which contains only a picnic area and parking lot. It adjoins the much larger Snyder Middleswarth National Natural Landmark and the large Tall Timbers Natural Area. This is a low-water hike. The trees are protected because they fall within the boundaries of the Snyder Middleswarth National Natural Landmark and the Tall Timbers Natural Area, parts of a 5700-hectare tract in Snyder County purchased by the state in 1902. Most of the big trees are hemlocks and a few are white pines. Because hemlock is brittle and may shatter when sawed into boards, it is not a profitable tree to log. This fact may have contributed to the owners' willingness to part with such a large tract containing hundreds of uncut hectares.

The hike begins in Snyder Middleswarth State Park, an area set aside for picnicking and parking. To reach the trailhead, turn north off PA 235 in Troxelville onto Swift Run Road, where there's a large sign for the park. Follow Swift Run Road for 4.7 miles, passing Rock Springs Picnic Area, to the entrance and parking area. Walking shoes are fine for this hike's good trail and short stretch of road.

You begin hiking on the Tall Timbers Trail, which leads upstream from the parking area, and immediately encounter the big trees. This is the way the land looked from lakes to sea 200 years ago. Bypass the trail on your left at 670 meters, which leads back to the park on the opposite bank of Swift Run. After 2 km Tower Trail cuts off to the left across Swift Run. This critical junction is marked only by a metal post on the right. (Should you miss this junction, you will find the trail deteriorates rapidly in blowdowns and brush and the big trees come to an abrupt end in 500 meters.)

Tall Timbers Trail

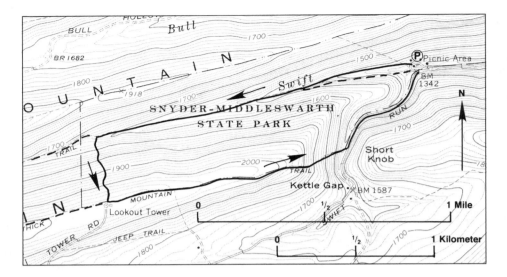

Turn left onto Tower Trail, cross Swift Run on some rocks, and start up the north flank of Thick Mountain. Bear right on the first switchback. The switchbacks are in good shape and offer easier climbing than the cutoff, which is starting to erode. This is the only real climb on the hike.

At the ridgetop you see four foundation posts at the end of a road. They are all that remain of Snyder Middleswarth fire tower. Views from the tower must have been fine, but the structure was a victim of state economy measures and the vandalism that still afflicts other towers.

You now turn left on the blue-blazed Thick Mountain Trail and follow the crest of the ridge past the site of an air crash that occurred on November 18, 1980. The plane was carrying *The New York Times* and apparently crashed into the ridgetop at full speed, killing the pilot. You soon begin your descent into Kettle Gap, moving from a gradual to a steep slope fairly rapidly. Toward the bottom you bear left on an old road grade and then cross an underground stream. You can hear the water flowing under the rocks.

The trail brings you out onto Swift Run Road, and you should turn left downhill. Walk about 500 meters and turn left on the road into Snyder Middleswarth picnic area. Cross Swift Run and you are back at your car.

17

Wykoff Run Natural Area

Distance: 7.8 km (4.8 miles)

Time: 2¾ hours

Vertical Rise: 85 meters (280 ft)

Highlights: White birch

Maps: USGS 7.5′ Devils Elbow, Driftwood; Quehanna Trail map

Wykoff Run Natural Area in the 20,000-hectare Quehanna Wild Area near Karthaus was established to preserve a beautiful stand of white birch. But as you drive to the trailhead and take this hike you see evidence of other use before the legislature declared it the state's largest wild area.

The state made heroic efforts to attract industry to this part of Clearfield and Cameron Counties when it showed signs of economic recession after World War II. It was successful with the Curtiss-Wright Aircraft Company, which wanted a secluded area to build jet engines and experiment with nuclear-powered aircraft. To satisfy the company's requirements, hunting camps were removed from a 20,000-hectare tract of state forest land and entrance was forbidden to all outsiders.

But things went badly for Curtiss-Wright. The region's unemployed coal miners knew nothing about jet engines and nuclear-powered aircraft, so engineers and scientists were imported to work and live in the company town of Pine Glen. The industrial venture soon failed. Curtiss-Wright abandoned the jet engine field and nuclear-powered aircraft never got off the ground. Piper Aircraft Company used some buildings but closed in 1984. A 4-megawatt research reactor has been converted to a cobalt-60 irradiation facility, which is still in operation. A boot camp for minimum security prisoners has been established at Piper. The rest of the area has reverted to deer, bears, rattlesnakes, and occasional hikers.

To reach the trailhead, drive up the Quehanna Highway from PA 879 in Karthaus for 8.7 miles to the junction with paved Wykoff Run Road, or drive 9.9 miles on Wykoff Run Road from PA 120 at Sinnemahoning. There is parking space for several cars at the junction of the two roads. Hiking boots are best for the hike described here.

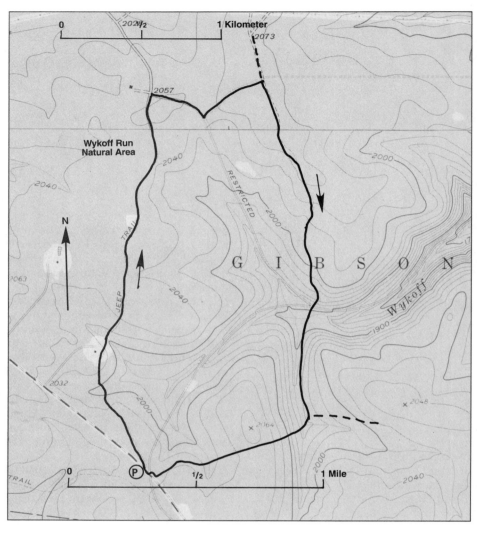

The blue-blazed Old Hoover Road, which is also a ski-touring trail, bisects the angle between the two roads. Some 600 meters from your start, you cross a dry run; a short distance beyond you enter a clearing. Here stands a concrete test cell for jet engines, which was later converted to the storage of hazardous and explosive materials. Now it has become a substrate for spray paint. Continue ahead and cross another small stream, probably the headwaters of Wykoff Run.

At 1.2 km you enter the grove of white birch trees. The trail is also lined with abundant mountain laurels, which bloom about the middle of June. At about 1.8 km you see a large clearing to your left. This is the beryllium oxide burial site. Monitoring wells have been drilled here to see if this material enters the ground water.

Butterflies dining on thistle

This is typical of Pennsylvania's wilderness: The land has been used and abused, sometimes repeatedly, but it keeps coming back.

At 2.7 km you reach Hoover Road and turn right. After 350 meters turn left onto a gated logging road. Both these roads are blue-blazed. At 3.5 km turn right on the blue-blazed Bailey Log Trail. There is a bear-chewed post sign at this junction, which does not mention this trail by name. Neverthless it is a pleasant trail with more white birch all the way to its intersection with Wykoff Run and Hoover Roads at 5.2 km.

Cross Wykoff Run Road and continue on a trail marked "Ski Trail," crossing a footbridge over Wykoff Run. This turns out to be the Big Spring Draft Trail and it is marked with both blue and white blazes. You pass through a stand of spruce, then enter a fairly open meadow. At 6.2 km you turn right on the Wykoff Trail at a sign that says "Quehanna Hwy 1." Cross two small streams as best you can; continue across a woods road and through a clearing to reach the Quehanna Highway. Turn right and another 100 meters brings you back to your car.

A free map of the Quehanna Trail and Wild Area can be obtained by writing to Moshannon State Forest, PO Box 952, Clearfield, PA 16830.

18

Jackson Trail

Distance: 10.1 km (6.3 miles)	
Time: 4¾ hours	
Vertical Rise: 280 meters (920 ft)	
Highlights: Views	
Maps: USGS 7.5' McAlevys Fort, Pine Grove Mills; MSTA Map 202.1	

The Jackson Trail is named for Evelyn Jackson, a former president of the Hiking Division of the Penn State Outing Club, under whose leadership many records of participation in PSOC activities were set—records that stand to this day. The Jackson Trail follows Tussey Ridge and is one of the most scenic trails near State College; however, the footway on Tussey Ridge varies from unusually rocky to nothing but rocks, rocks, and more rocks. Hiking boots are in order for this circuit hike, but the trailhead is on a paved highway so it is available year-round. This hike should be reserved for clear weather so the many views will not be wasted.

Tussey Ridge is formed by a hard layer of sandstone called the Tuscarora. Here it forms one side of an anticline or upfold formed when North America collided with Africa several hundred million years ago. The other side of this fold is Bald Eagle Mountain, visible to the north and west along this hike. In between these ridges the Tuscarora arched high over what is now Nittany Valley. Other rocks, which can now be seen in the Allegheny Front beyond Bald Eagle, covered the Tuscarora. In all, a thickness of 10 km of rock has been removed by erosion from Nittany Valley.

The trailhead is the same one used for Hike 26. It is the parking area on PA 26, 2 miles uphill from the intersection with PA 45 in Pine Grove Mills.

On this hike you must cross the paved highway and bear left on the gated jeep road along the top of Tussey Ridge. Be sure that you are following a blue-blazed trail. A sign identifies the Jackson Trail. Soon you pass the last antenna with which hikers share the ridgetops. Despite the inevitable access road, the antennas are preferable to the far more invasive power-producing windmills that will line these ridges in the future.

Now your route becomes a real trail that follows a survey swath to a USGS triangulation marker reached at 1.1 km. A few steps farther brings you to an over-

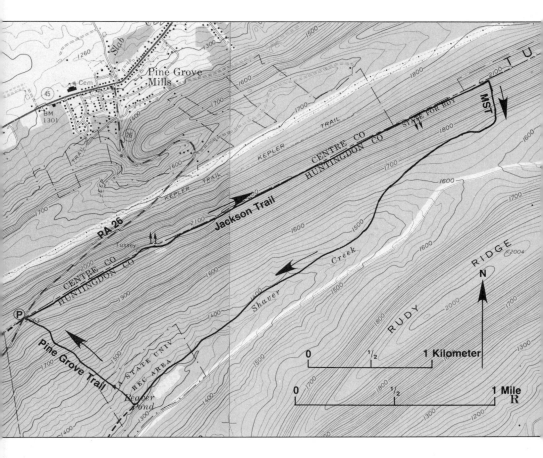

look to the south. The view from this side of the ridge is a wild one, with heavily wooded Rudy Ridge on the far side of Pine Swamp Valley. A view to the north quickly follows, angled away from State College; you can see Bald Eagle Ridge and the Allegheny Front beyond the wooded barrens.

At 1.6 km you reach Lone Pine—a single white pine growing out of the rocky crest of Tussey Mountain. You come to a rare stretch of good footway at 1.9 km. Treasure it as it is all too short. Soon the footway reverts to rocks and you reach more views to the south and over Rudy Ridge. You hike several more sec-

tions of good footway before reaching a corner of private land at 3.4 km. The border of state forest land is marked by the white paint blazes and the trail endeavors to stay on the public side of the line. Extensive views to the south soon follow but at places all traces of footway vanish and you must make your way over the rocks as best you can. Hubler Gap, between Kocher Mountain and Rudy Ridge, has now come into view. Since this ridge is also formed by the Tuscarora sandstone, faulting is indicated with a vertical displacement of the Tuscarora.

At 4.5 km you reach a junction with the orange-blazed Mid State Trail (MST).

Spring along Mid State Trail in Pine Swamp Valley

Turn right and descend steeply over rocks. Caution—in wet weather these rocks can be very slippery. The trail then picks up some log skids, presumably used by the Linden Hall Lumber Company around the turn of the century. At the bottom of the slope, the trail turns right along the base of the ridge and at one point passes through a recent logging operation.

After passing a pair of springs, bear right on an old charcoal road at 6.5 km. This road can be traced all the way to Monroe Furnace on PA 26. Monroe Furnace operated from the 1830s until after the Civil War, but its charcoal roads have been used in logging operations since then.

At 6.8 km, you pass the first of three sawmill sites used in the mid-1960s, and at 8.3 km, you pass in front of a hunting camp. Just beyond the camp there is a spring to the left of the trail. The Mid State Trail then traverses the former Beaver Pond Recreation Area, passing a side trail to Garbage Bag Spring. A major trail junction is reached at 8.9 km. Ahead, the blue-blazed Ironstone Loop leads to Stone Valley Recreation Area, but you turn right on the Pine Grove Trail for the climb back up Tussey Mountain to the parking lot on PA 26.

Other hiking opportunities in the area include Hike 26 on the Indian Steps and the Ironstone Loop Trail. The latter makes an all-day bootbuster of 23 km length.

19

Greenwood Fire Tower

Distance: 10.5 km (6.5 miles)

Time: 4 hours

Vertical Rise: 425 meters (1400 ft)

Highlights: Views from fire tower; charcoal iron furnace

Maps: USGS 7.5' McAlevys Fort, Barrville; PSOC Map 203

A mountain panorama and a glimpse of the early iron industry await you on this hike. Charcoal furnaces, the relics of which you see along here, provided the country with iron from before the Revolution until late in the 19th century. The intense industrial activity that existed at this now peaceful location began in 1837, and the site's Greenwood Furnace continued operations until December 1904. It was one of the longest operating charcoal iron furnaces in the country.

Your hike starts and ends at Greenwood Furnace State Park on PA 305, which is 5 miles east of the junction with PA 26 at McAlevys Fort in Stone Valley. You can park in the lot next to park head-

quarters at the junction of PA 305 and Black Lick Road. Hiking boots are in order for this hike.

Begin walking down Black Lick Road. Almost immediately a large mound with trees growing from it appears on your right. The large stone structure behind it is the rebuilt replica of Stack 2 at Greenwood Furnace. An archaeological excavation has revealed the location of Stack 1 off to the side. The siting of these furnaces called for a source of iron ore. The high-grade ore used here came from the hematite quarries on Brush Ridge west of the park. More importantly, the furnace had to be located in a vast tract of forest that could supply charcoal to smelt the ore. As most level land near here had been cleared for farming, only the steeper mountainsides were still forested. Water power was also required to run the air blast.

The production of charcoal was handled by woodsmen and colliers. First the woodsman had to carve a level area called a coal hearth or charcoal flat from the mountainside. You will see several of these flats as you climb up Broad Mountain. The woodsman also had to make a wagon road from one flat to another so the charcoal could be transported to the iron furnace. You will follow such old

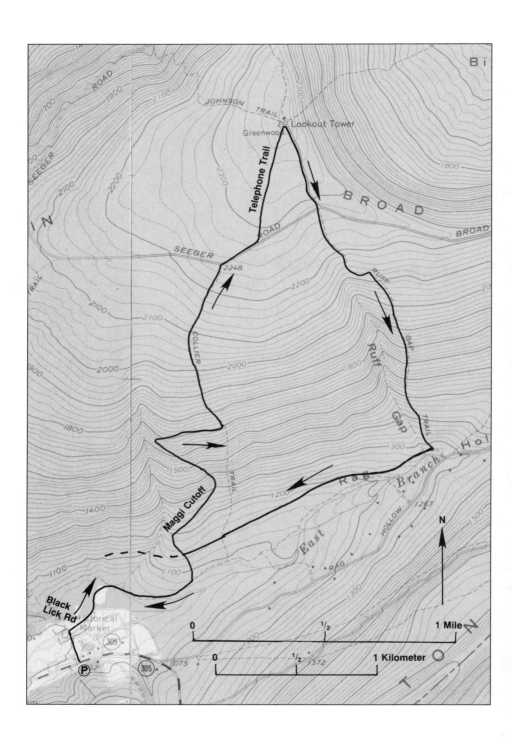

Replica of Greenwood Furnace Stack 2

charcoal roads in several places. Once a new flat was built, the woodsman had to cut, split, and stack all the trees in the vicinity. At this point, the collier took over and covered the stack with earth and/or wet leaves and set it afire. Now came the long and lonely time as the collier tended the fire for 10 days to 2 weeks. If the fire didn't get enough air it went out and had to be rekindled. If it received too much air, the entire stack would burn to worthless ash.

Even when the stack was finally converted to charcoal the collier had to wait until it had cooled enough so it would not reignite when opened to the air. When the furnace operated, it consumed the charcoal from a hectare of woodland every day.

Charcoal operations eventually reached as far as Big Flat and even across Thickhead Mountain down into Bear Meadows. The end did not come from competition with high-grade ore from the Mesabi Range in Minnesota, but from exhaustion of the forests during the first decade of this century when the furnace was competing with several logging railroad operations for the few remaining trees.

Continue on Black Lick Road across Standing Stone Creek, and turn right on the blue-blazed Greenwood Spur of the Mid State Trail. Head across the meadow and into the woods. Here you wander east past more ruins and some very large white pines, then along several old roads, and across a small run. Bear left and begin climbing, shortly crossing a charcoal flat with wild dogwood growing on it. Make careful note of the crossing of a bulldozed snowmobile trail, as you will need to find this junction on your way back. Turn right at the next charcoal flat.

Now begins a steep climb up Broad Mountain on an old charcoal road. At 2.9 km the Greenwood Spur turns left on the Collier Trail. By the time you reach Seeger Road the grade has leveled. Follow the blazes right for some 200 meters and then bear left on the Telephone Trail to the base of Greenwood Fire Tower.

If the day is clear the views from the tower are spectacular. To the north is Indian Wells Overlook above Bear Meadows and Little Flat Fire Tower (see Hike 25). Thickhead Mountain stands with the microwave relay at its east end. Stone Gap, Grass Mountain, Slate Ridge, Long Mountain, and the other Broad Mountain are together, with upper Stone Valley and Stone Mountain itself bending off toward the horizon. Jacks Mountain is the one with the conspicuous gap to the side of Milligan's Knob. On a really clear day you may see Shade Mountain beyond the Juniata.

It appears that Ruff Gap Trail and the snowmobile trail may be opened to mountain bikes and horses. If you wish to avoid encounters with these trail users, return to Greenwood Furnace State Park the way you came.

To return by a different route, leave the blazes and follow the tower access road to its junction with Seeger and Broad Mountain Roads. From here bear slightly to the right and continue into the woods on the unmarked but obvious Ruff Gap Trail. This trail appears to be another old charcoal road and passes several more flats on its way down into Rag Hollow. Near the bottom you reach the corner of a recent clear-cut that provides a view down Rag Hollow. To avoid walking on Rag Hollow Road and PA 305, turn right on a logging road near the bottom of the clear-cut. Follow it across the clear-cut to a log landing near the far side.

Continue on a snowmobile trail that soon enters the woods. Turn left on the blue-blazed Greenwood Spur and retrace your steps to your car. (If you miss this junction the snowmobile trail will bring you out on Black Lick Road.)

Other hiking opportunities at Greenwood Furnace State Park can be found on the Link Trail (Charcoal Path), which climbs Stone Mountain to the south of PA 305.

20

Yost Run

Distance: 11.4 km (7.1 miles)

Time: 4¾ hours

Vertical Rise: 395 meters (1295 ft)

Highlights: Waterfall

Maps: USGS 7.5' Snow Shoe NW; Chuck Keiper Trail map

A waterfall in the remote depths of Yost Run Canyon is the attraction on this part of the Chuck Keiper Trail. The trail, opened in 1977, is a memorial to Charles F. Keiper, conservationist and sportsman, who was the district game protector in western Clinton County for 22 years. The commemoration is a singular tribute to a law enforcement officer.

Another feature of this hike is the large clear-cuts resulting from devastation by the oak leaf roller from 1968 to 1972. This native insect underwent a population explosion and repeatedly defoliated the large stands of oak on the Allegheny Plateau. The oak mortality ranged from 50 to 100 percent over many thousands of hectares. The clear-

cuts on this hike and along PA 144 are salvage cuts designed to save as much timber and pulpwood as possible and to reduce the forest fire hazard resulting from such vast stands of dead trees. The clear-cuts have been slow to revegetate into trees because there are few, if any, stump sprouts.

Along this hike and others in Sproul State Forest keep your eyes open for a weasel-like animal that reaches a length of over a meter and a weight of up to 6 kg. This is the fisher, which is being reintroduced into Penn's Woods after an absence of over a century. Fishers are predators that eat mice, shrews, squirrels, and porcupines—but not fish—so their name is a bit of a mystery. They are obtained from New Hampshire and the Adirondacks. Porcupines, their prey, eat tree bark (often killing the tree) as well as trail signs and bridges; we can certainly spare a few porcupines to welcome the fishers back.

Due to repeated stream crossings this is a trail best hiked when water levels are low. You must step on rocks or wade across. You will want your hiking boots for the stream crossings.

The trailhead for this hike is on PA 144, 13.4 miles northeast from the intersection with PA 879 near Moshannon.

You can also reach it by driving 17.2 miles south on PA 144 from the junction with PA 120 in Renovo. There is plenty of parking space in a borrow pit on the northwest side of the highway, 0.1 mile south of the Eddy Lick Trail.

You begin by hiking north along the highway to the unblazed but signed Eddy Lick Trail and then turning left. The trail, which here is actually a jeep road that leads to several hunting camps, quickly enters an extensive salvage cut. You move straight across the clear-cut, go through a narrow band of trees, and then cross another salvage cut. At 2.2 km you reach the Chuck Keiper Trail at Crystal Spring Hunting Camp, 10-C-30. During the lumbering days early in this century a logging camp was located here. The horse stables were near the spring and the bunkhouses were about 800 meters down Second Fork Trail. Circle around the camp on the trail and start your descent down the second fork of Yost Run. This trail is marked with yellow blazes of variable sizes and shapes. A double blaze means a turn or stream crossing. The second fork soon begins to cut a spectacular gash of its own, leaving you and the trail high above on the steep, rocky slope. Near the end, the trail switches back down to streamside.

At 4.6 km you reach Yost Run and turn upstream, where you begin to encounter the chutes and cascades of this beautiful stream. You cross Yost Run six times and then cross a smaller side stream from Log Hollow on your left. This is followed by eight more crossings

Ledges along Yost Run

of the run. At 8.5 km the Kyler Fork comes in on the far side of the run and just beyond you reach the waterfall. True, the fall's total drop is only 4 meters, but waterfalls of even this modest size are rare in unglaciated regions. Presumably, the fall exists due to a layer of unusually resistant rock.

Complete your hike by following the blazes upstream and turning left up Bloom Draft in front of Hunting Camp 10-C-244. (*Draft* in this sense is an archaic American usage meaning a gulch or canyon.) After you pass Camp Bloom, 10-C-23, you reach a vehicle gate at a junction of woods roads. Here, the Chuck Keiper Trail turns right on a haul road but you go straight ahead on an unblazed old woods road that brings you out on PA 144 at 10.8 km. Turn left along the highway and keep to the left—facing traffic—for the walk back to your car.

You can obtain a copy of the Chuck Keiper Trail map by writing to Sproul State Forest, HCR 62, Box 90, Renovo, PA 17764. For a camping permit call 717-923-1450.

21

Rock Run Trail

Distance: 11.6 km (7.2 miles)

Time: 4¼ hours

Vertical Rise: 190 meters (620 ft)

Highlights: Mountain stream, logging railroad grades

Maps: USGS 7.5' Bear Knob; Rock Run Trail map

With the popularity of cross-country skiing, volunteer groups have cut and blazed new trails. Although forestry roads would be ideal for cross-country skiing, these roads are used by snow machines and four-wheel-drive vehicles during the winter; hence the need for new trails. Pennsylvania's climate is marginal for skiing, which skiers acknowledge by saying they ski in the "banana belt." Every meter of altitude helps to increase the snowpack in Penn's Woods. The Rock Run Trail, visited on this hike, was built by the Cross Country Ski Division of the Penn State Outing Club on the Allegheny Front to take advantage of some of the highest elevations around. These elevations vary from 520 to 730 meters, not very high even for the Appalachians, but the best available. You are welcome to hike or even backpack the Rock Run Trail when there is no snow cover. Postholing (walking in deep snow without skis or snowshoes; with every step you dig another posthole) would of course ruin the ski tracks should there be enough snow for skiing. The rest of the year, your hiking helps to keep down the brush.

The trailhead for this hike is at the junction of PA 504 and Tram Road. This point is 4.5 miles east of the Julian Pike in Black Moshannon State Park, and 7.2 miles west of US 220 at Unionville. There is some parking space on the south side of the highway opposite the trailhead. You will want your hiking boots because of the occasionally rocky footway, the stream crossings, and wet spots.

To start this hike, pick up the blue-blazed Entrance Trail at the sign on the other side of PA 504. Cross a pipeline and then bear right on a logging road that leads over a low hill and into an extensive oak-leaf-roller salvage cut. Since the trees were killed before they were cut, this area has been slow to revegetate. The spruce that were planted here have only done well in spots.

Rock Run Trail

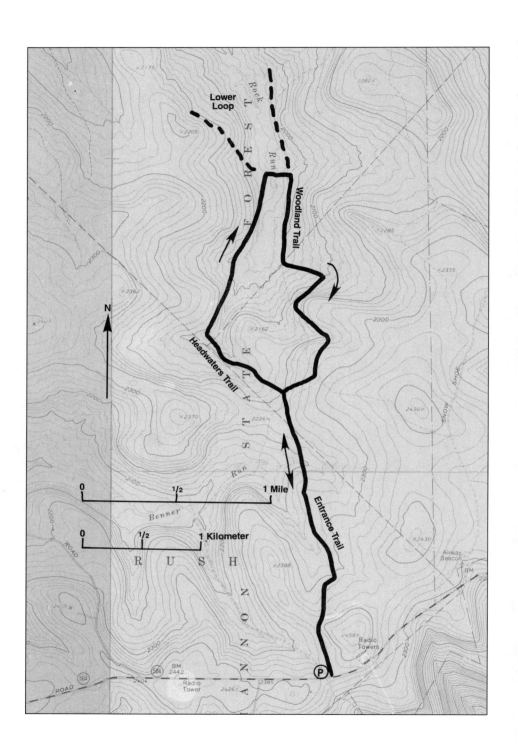

Lower
Loop

Woodland
Trail

Headwaters Trail

N

0   1/2   1 Mile

0   1/2   1 Kilometer

Entrance Trail

R   U   S   H   O   N

Benner

ROAD

504

BM
2442

Radio
Tower

ROAD

Radio
Towers

Airway
Beacon

BM

P

At 1.0 km turn right at a post sign; you soon enter the woods. Next you cross a bridge over the headwaters of Benner Run. Along this stretch you may see evidence of acid rain research in progress. After passing through a scrub oak stand you cross a woods road and at 3.1 km you reach a junction with the upper loop of Rock Run Trail. There is a trail register at this junction. Please register. Then turn left on the Headwaters Trail and follow it across several streams, the last of which has a bridge. This trail is narrow and has sharp turns designed to discourage use by snow machines, so watch the blazes carefully. You pick up an old logging railroad grade at 4.0 km. According to Benjamin Kline in his book *Pitch Pine and Prop Timber*, Rock Run was logged by a J.W. Beecher of Sober, in Centre County. The location of this community is not shown on current maps but it was probably named for a partner in the firm, C.K. Sober, rather than for the teetotaling proclivities of its inhabitants.

Follow the old grade until it disappears. Then watch carefully for an obscure jog to the left. You reach a junction of trails at 5.7 km. The lower loop bears left on the Ridge Trail but you turn right and cross a footbridge over Rock Run. The bridge has been attacked by porcupines in recent years. Next pass a junction with the Valley Trail that forms the other half of the lower loop. Then bear right on another old tram road. This is the Woodland Trail. You cross a jeep road and several small streams, but at 7.0 km you turn left off the old grade and proceed through the woods on trail. Ignore a white-blazed trail at 7.3 km; continue instead on the Headwaters Trail to a junction with a jeep road, which you cross.

At 8.6 km you reach the junction with the Entrance Trail. Turn left and retrace your steps to your car on PA 504.

Additional hiking opportunities are available on the lower loop of the Rock Run Trail and at Black Moshannon State Park (Hike 28). The Rock Run Trail map is available from Moshannon State Forest, PO Box 952, Clearfield, PA 16830. For a camping permit call 814-765-3741.

22

Eddy Lick Run

Distance: 11.8 km (7.3 miles)

Time: 4¼ hours

Vertical Rise: 290 meters (950 ft)

Highlights: Splash dam

Maps: USGS 7.5' Snow Shoe NE; Chuck Keiper Trail map

Traces of a splash dam and a logging railroad make this hike on the West Loop of the Chuck Keiper Trail a historic trek. A splash dam permitted logging along streams that were too small to float logs even in the spring flood. Most splash dams were temporary affairs made of logs and earth, but the one on Eddy Lick Run was built largely of rock and may be the best preserved in the state.

Toward the end of the 19th century the development of steam-powered geared locomotives allowed logging where the streams were too small even for splash dams. Such locomotives were run at the lowest gear in order to provide the greatest power and traction. In this way grades of up to 15 percent could be negotiated with even a couple of log cars.

But the price of the feat was the sacrifice of speed; such locomotives were limited to about 25 km per hour flat out.

By the early part of this century, geared locomotives were being built by three different manufacturers in weights of 10 to over 100 tons. Today a museum at Corry, Pennsylvania, has the only Climax locomotive, and the Pennsylvania Lumber Museum at Denton Hill State Park the only Shay locomotive, left in the state. You must visit the Cass Scenic Railroad at Cass, West Virginia, if you want to see a geared locomotive in operation.

The trailhead for this hike is on De Hass Road, 0.2 mile from PA 144. On PA 144 De Hass Road is 15 miles northeast from the junction with PA 879 near Moshannon or 15.5 miles south from the junction with PA 120 in Renovo. Park where the pipeline crosses De Hass Road. This hike is best taken during the low-water season due to the many stream crossings on Eddy Lick Run. Wear your hiking boots on this hike.

Start by heading southwest down the pipeline swath toward Dry Run. The pipeline has been fenced off to cars and trucks, but it is still used by motorcycles, ATVs, and other off-road vehicles; you can see evidence of their deleterious effects in the water-soaked soil of Dry Run Hollow.

Old logging railroad grade

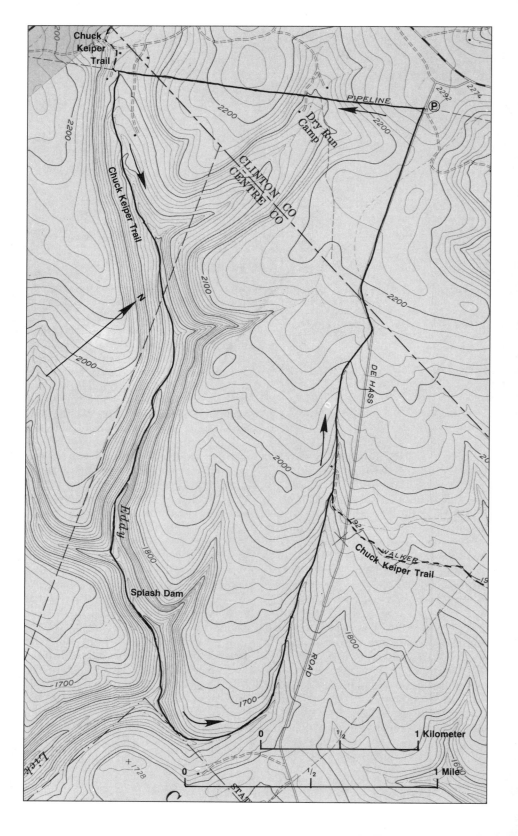

After picking your way across and around the muddy spots, you climb the next hill through an oak-leaf-roller salvage cut. In the second valley you cross Eddy Lick Run for the first time and turn left, downstream, following the yellow blazes of the Chuck Keiper Trail. In places the trail has been cut into the side of the valley, while in others it follows closely along the stream bank. After six crossings of Eddy Lick Run the trail meets and turns left on an old logging railroad grade. You can tell this is an old railroad grade and not a haul or skid road by the uniformity of its grade, its lack of sharp turns, and the frequent and regularly spaced transverse depressions formed where the ties rotted in place.

In about 50 meters the railroad grade crosses a side stream. The bridge is long gone, but some of its old timbers can still be seen in the streambed. Another 200 meters brings you to the old splash dam. The railroad grade is cut through a corner of the dam, thus rendering it useless. The spillway is at the far side and a few old timbers remain. In use, the pond behind the dam was allowed to fill while logs were piled in front of the spillway. All trees and brush were cleared from the valley below so that logs wouldn't be impeded. When all was ready, the spillway gate opened and the flood picked up the logs and carried them away. Crews of men ran along both sides of the stream to refloat stranded logs before the splash was over. It was a labor-intensive method of bringing logs to a sawmill.

After you investigate the old dam, continue along the trail. Note the large white pine that has grown in the middle of the old railroad grade. It has been a long time since any trains passed this way! Soon you cross Eddy Lick Run on a footbridge at the ruins of the old railroad bridge. This bridge shows conclusively that the splash dam was not used after the railroad was built; had a splash full of logs hit this bridge it would have made an awful mess.

Shortly beyond the old bridge site you bear left and start the long climb back to the plateau. The white blazes here mark the boundary of Sproul State Forest, not the trail, so stick with the yellow blazes. After 400 meters you bear left along a jeep road. When it curves right you can see you are on another old railroad grade. This grade also appears to be standard gauge, so it probably was a spur of the one back in Eddy Lick Run. Logging railroads were built in a wide variety of gauges. The advantage of standard gauge was that log cars could go straight onto any regular railroad and be hauled to a distant sawmill. However, in early logging operations narrow gauges and the slow speed of geared locomotives meant sawmills had to be close to cutting sites.

At 9.1 km the Chuck Keiper Trail turns off the old railroad grade and quickly turns right on a jeep road. To reach your car turn left here and follow the jeep trail for about 250 meters to its end at a hunting camp. In front of the camp bear right on the same old railroad grade. Follow it as it continues its gentle climb past a small pond and spring and finally a white pine plantation. Here you bear right on a logging road that has been built over the railroad grade.

At 10.3 km bear left on De Hass Road. It is 1.6 km back to your car at the pipeline. Notice that the old railroad grade continues on the far side of De Hass Road but is heavily overgrown.

You can obtain a copy of the Chuck Keiper Trail map by writing to Sproul State Forest, HCR 62, Box 90, Renovo, PA 17764. Call 717-923-1450 for a camping permit.

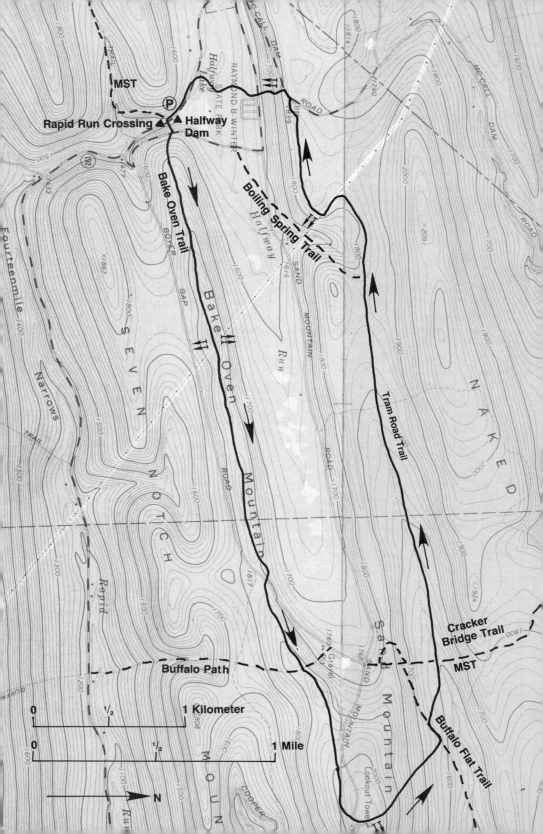

23

Sand Mountain Tower

Distance: 12.7 km (7.9 miles)

Time: 4½ hours

Vertical Rise: 360 meters (1180 ft)

Highlights: Fire tower, views

Maps: USGS 7.5' Carroll, Hartleton

For much of its route, this circuit hike follows the Halfway cross-country ski trail east of Raymond B. Winter State Park. The *Halfway* name derives from the park's location halfway through the 14-mile narrows. During the latter part of the 19th century, livestock was driven east through this narrows to the railroad at Lewisburg. A tavern at this location provided overnight lodgings for the herders—a very civilized arrangement in comparison with western cattle drives. In the 1930s, the Civilian Conservation Corps built the Halfway Dam. The Halfway ski trail is a pleasantly varied route following ridges some places and stream valleys elsewhere. A couple of variations take in Sand Mountain Fire Tower and avoid most of McCall Dam Road.

Raymond B. Winter State Park is located on PA 192 about 20 miles west of Lewisburg, just east of the Centre-Union County line. The trailhead is the parking lot adjacent to Halfway Dam on PA 192, but any other parking lot in the park could be used. You will want your hiking boots for this trail as the old logging railroad grades are mostly rocks. Clearly, you should avoid this trail if there is enough snow for skiing. You would ruin the ski tracks and get only an exhausting slog in return. Any other time of year this trail will reward your efforts, be it with flowering shadbush in the spring or fall foliage in the autumn.

To start the hike, walk east along the lakeshore, passing the dam. Cross Rapid Run very carefully on the PA 192 bridge and turn sharp left just beyond, picking up the orange-blazed Mid State Trail (MST). At the corner of the dam, you get a last view of the swimming beach backed by Naked Mountain. See the overlook on Naked Mountain? You will visit it near the end of this hike.

Turn sharp right and climb a set of old stone steps to the paved park road. Here you continue on the Bake Oven Trail. This is the steepest climb on the hike, but after a few hundred meters it eases off and you are on the crest of

Mid State Trail on Bake Oven Ridge

Bake Oven Mountain, where an abundance of hemlocks and white pines make this a delightful trail.

You pass the old Park Boundary Trail at 1.2 km, and after some stands of white birch reach the new park boundary where the Pennsylvania Power & Light power line crosses the ridge. Here there are views of Chestnut Flat and Boiling Springs Gap to the left and Jones Mountain to the right, across Seven Notch Mountain. A sharp drop just ahead provides thrills for cross-country skiers. At 3.3 km you reach another view to the south. This one has been inadvertently provided by firewood cutters in their ever-widening search for dead trees. Next, you cross Boyer Gap Road and continue on relatively new trail cut by the Youth Conservation Corps in 1979.

A junction with the blue-blazed Buffalo Path is reached at 4.3 km. The ski trail turns left here but you continue east on the orange-blazed Mid State Trail. Despite the many Buffalo Trails, Flats, and Runs there is no hard evidence that buffalo ever lived in this part of the state. They failed to leave any bones, horns, or teeth. Nobody ever reported their presence in a letter or journal. However, the November 1994 issue of *National Geographic* does show the buffalo's range extending east all the way to the Delaware River back in 1500.

Next you turn left on a pole line, cross Sand Mountain Road, and reach Sand Mountain Fire Tower at 5.7 km. The views from the top are extraordinary. To the west, you can see the valley where R.B. Winter State Park is located, but only a short stretch of PA 192 is visible. To the east, the curve of Buffalo Mountain plows through the lowlands along the Susquehanna like a giant ship. To the north, I-80 is hidden in one of the numerous folds of this crumpled terrain. The single open field you can see is on the far side of I-80.

Back on the trail, you follow the Mid State down the north flank of Sand Mountain picking up an old log skid partway down. At 6.5 km you turn left on the Buffalo Flat Trail, which is actually an old logging railroad grade of Monroe Kulp's Lewisburg operation.

Soon you rejoin the Halfway ski trail. Bear right off the railroad grade and descend to the edge of Spruce Run. It gradually becomes apparent that you are following another one of Monroe Kulp's far-flung railroad grades. Kulp favored a 3-foot narrow gauge. At 7.2 km there is a junction with the Cracker Bridge Trail. Here, the Mid State Trail turns right, but you continue ahead on the blue-blazed Tram Road Trail (which the sign mistakenly calls "Chestnut Flat Trail"). The name *Cracker Bridge* stems from a mishap on yet another of Kulp's railroads on the far side of Naked Mountain. The track was so rough that a barrel of crackers being carried to a logging camp bounced off and rolled down the mountainside.

About 100 meters beyond the Cracker Bridge Trail you cross the outlet from a large spring just to the left of the trail. Next, you begin a series of crossings of Spruce Run, all of which have new bridges. There is a good campsite on your left just before the first bridge. The stream becomes smaller at each crossing as you gradually climb to the height-of-land.

At 10.3 km the blue-blazed Boiling Spring Trail goes left to the park and provides a way to truncate your hike. Ahead you cross a jeep road and just beyond turn left on another jeep road under the PP&L power line. This jeep road brings you to the edge of Boiling Spring Gap and you can look across Halfway Run Valley to Bake Oven Mountain, where you hiked earlier.

Turn right into the woods and continue west along the edge of the mountain to 11.7 km where you bear left on

McCall Dam Road to the lookout over R.B. Winter State Park. Then find the Lookout Trail at the left corner of the platform and follow it downhill. Cross the paved park road at the bottom of the hill and follow a sign to the Nature Trail. Bear right at a trail junction and continue ahead on the white-blazed Nature Trail at the next junction. Then cross a pole-line swath and turn right at the edge of the lake. Cross a bridge and continue along the water's edge to the parking lot.

In season, you might take time for a swim. The lake is spring fed and even in August it feels great after a day's hike in Penn's Woods. Other hiking opportunities at R.B. Winter State Park can be found on the Mid State Trail west of the park. For a camping permit call Bald Eagle State Forest at 717-922-3344.

24

Hook Natural Area

Distance: 13.0 km (8.1 miles)

Time: 5 hours

Vertical Rise: 370 meters (1220 ft)

Highlights: Large natural area

Maps: USGS 7.5' Hartleton, Mifflinburg

The Hook Natural Area in Bald Eagle State Forest is the largest officially designated natural area in the state. Today it is approximately 2000 hectares of forest with a few trails used occasionally by hunters, hikers, and fishermen. But during the logging era at the turn of the century the hills were busy with railroads, log slides, trails, and haul roads.

The Hook Natural Area is in Bald Eagle State Forest between PA 192 and PA 45. To reach the start of this hike take SR 3005 north from the Christ United Lutheran Church on PA 45 between Hartleton and Mifflinburg. After driving 3.3 miles on this road, turn left on Diehl Road (T 372) and continue to the junction with the old Shingle Road. Use the parking area on the left at this junction.

For an alternative start off Jones Mountain Road, drive south on Pine Creek Road from its junction with PA 192 about 1 mile south of R.B. Winter State Park. After crossing the first ridge take Jones Mountain Road, on the left, as far as the junction with the Molasses Gap Trail, park your car, and begin hiking.

In either case you will want your hiking boots for this extra-vehicular activity.

If you park at the junction of old Shingle and Diehl Roads, start your hike by turning left on the road. Follow the road to the Mifflinburg Reservoir and then bear right on an old road just beyond the last reservoir building. After passing the berm, progress is slow as you are on an old, rocky railroad grade which is marked with blue-spot blazes. On your right the north branch of Buffalo Creek flows through a tunnel in the rhododendron, creating a challenge for anglers seeking native brook trout. The grade is overgrown in places with rhododendron and hemlock.

Next you pass a junction with the Knoll Ridge Trail. Then the Molasses Gap Trail comes down from Little Mountain at 4.4 km but this junction remains obscure. Continuing on the railroad grade, you soon cross a streambed coming from between Little and Dogback

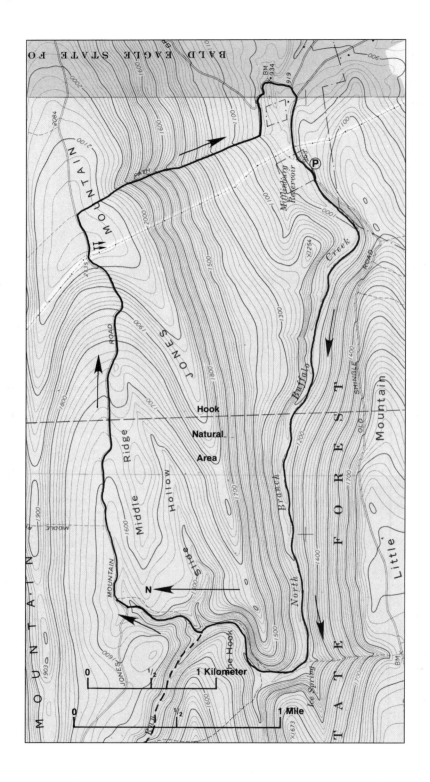

National Guard helicopter delivering new bridge for the Hook

Mountains. Ice Spring is on your left between the two streambeds but it flows only at the wettest times of the year.

In about 300 meters you cross the north branch of Buffalo Creek on stepping-stones. A footbridge is scheduled to be built at this crossing. Materials will be transported to the site by National Guard helicopter. Before you come to Panther Run the trail swings right to avoid further stream crossings. The trail tunnels through rhododendrons and passes several large white pines. Continue past a junction with the Middle Ridge Trail at Slide Hollow. After another 100 meters turn right on Molasses Gap Trail toward Jones Mountain Road. Avoid the Mule Shanty Trail which continues up Panther Run. The Molasses Gap Trail follows another rocky railroad grade. Where this grade becomes brush-covered, turn left onto Jones Mountain Road just ahead.

Head to the right on the road, past an excellent piped spring (here is your last chance to refill your canteen), and climb gently but steadily for 3 km to the power line atop Jones Mountain. Walk south along the power line to the mountain edge for a view of farmlands to the south and Penn's Creek Mountain in the distance. The rise at the far side of the power-line swath offers a view of mountains to the west.

To descend Jones Mountain, continue east on Jones Mountain Road for 300 meters and turn right onto Buffalo Path, which is marked with blue rectangles. Legend says this path was a migration route for buffalo moving south from Nippenose Valley. Despite all the mountains, valleys, creeks, and paths labeled "Buffalo," the buffalo legend seems difficult to substantiate. No written records show buffalo existed in the state, nor has evidence been discovered of buffalo bones, horns or teeth. The November 1994 issue of *National Geographic*, however, shows the historic range of buffalo extending all the way east to the Delaware River!

The path is fairly straight, although a bit overgrown in places. About 900 meters after you start down Buffalo Path a spring surfaces in the middle of the trail. It disappears and resurfaces as you move down the mountain, and sometimes you can hear it running deep under the rocks.

At the mountain base the slope eases and the path becomes a woods road.

Turn left onto the Knoll Ridge Trail, which is a jeep road at this point. Cross a stream, and turn right on the intersecting Brandon Road. Bear right at a subsequent intersection and you are soon back at your car. Be aware that camping is not permitted in the Hook Natural Area, as it is the catchment area for a public water supply system.

Further hiking opportunities nearby can be found at R.B. Winter State Park on PA 192 (Hike 23).

25

Little Flat

Distance: 13.9 km (8.6 miles)	
Time: 5¾ hours	
Vertical Rise: 260 meters (850 ft)	
Highlights: Views, fire tower	
Maps: USGS 7.5' State College, McAlevys Fort; PSOC Map 203	

In the Seven Mountains region near State College lies an unusual bog known as the Bear Meadows Natural Area. As this region was never glaciated, Bear Meadows is not a northern bog but rather a type usually found in the southern United States. The meadows are thought to have been created by beavers in a region of poor drainage about 10,000 years ago. Although the pond formed by their dams covered over 120 hectares, it was shallow. Over the intervening millennia it has filled with peat, and microscopic examination of cores taken from the area shows the nature of the ghost forests of the past. Spruce pollen in the bottom layers indicates that at the height of the last ice age these ridges were covered with spruce forests, or taigas, such as those found in Siberia and northern Canada today. As the ice retreated, spruce gave way to pine, and it, in turn, gave way to the richly diverse forests found by the colonists. Many unusual plant species are found in the bog, including carnivorous plants and specimens of red and black spruce as well as clumps of highbush blueberry. You are welcome to explore the meadows but prepare for wet feet and take a compass, as it is easy to get "turned around" there. This hike follows much drier trails, affording repeated views of the meadows from the surrounding ridges.

The beginning of the trail is 3.7 driving miles from the junction of Bear Meadows Road and US 322 east of Boalsburg. Follow Bear Meadows Road south past Tussey Mountain Ski Resort and through Galbraith Gap. Once through the gap, take the first road right, just after a small pond. This is Laurel Run Road and you follow it up the northern flank of Tussey Mountain. The road duplicates the route of the Linden Hall Lumber Company's narrow-gauge logging railroad and is therefore narrow, so be sure to honk as you approach each of the three blind curves. The outside loop at the second switchback is reputed to be

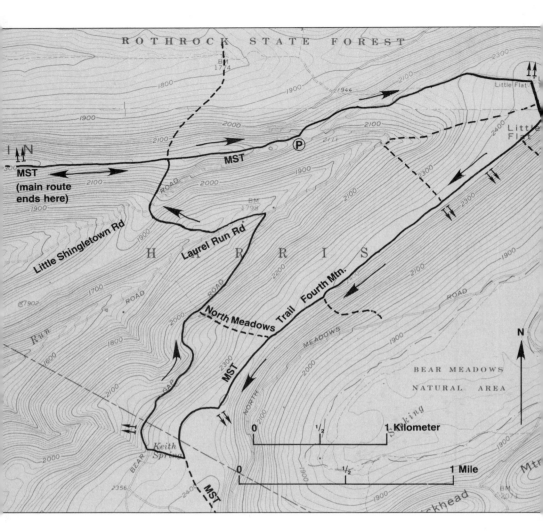

the sharpest turn on any road in the state.

Park at the top of the ridge where you reach the Mid State Trail crossing (don't block the gate on the Little Shingletown fire road). Due to the often rocky footway, you will want your hiking boots for this excursion.

Begin hiking left on the orange-blazed Mid State Trail (MST), proceeding along the exceedingly rocky railroad bed to the end of the last switchback.

Swing uphill to Little Flat Road (usually gated off) and bear left. Soon you reach an overlook with views of Bald Knob, Nittany Mountain, and Penn's Valley. Continue on the road past the junction with the Shingletown Trail to the base of Little Flat Fire Tower at 1.9 km. Little Flat Fire Tower is used during the high fire danger periods of April through May and October through November, when trees are bare and snow is absent.

Indian Wells Vista on Fourth Mountain

On a clear day, the tower views are extraordinary. Most of the State College urban area is discreetly concealed behind Bald Knob, but you can see Mount Nittany as well as Tussey Ridge, Thickhead Mountain, and Broad Mountain. To the east, Penn's Valley stretches to its end beyond Woodward. The isolated ridge in this valley is Egg Hill.

You now take the Mid State Trail, which here follows the Kettle Trail south into the woods from the base of Little Flat Tower. Shortly you intersect the Laurel Run and Spruce Gap Trails. Spruce Gap is an old name for Galbraith Gap but it is unlikely that spruce grew here. Except in acid bogs, spruce has not grown wild in Pennsylvania for many thousands of years. The many spruce-named gaps, runs, and mountains in Penn's Woods are likely due to mistaking hemlock for spruce.

The Kettle Trail soon turns off to the left; you continue ahead on the Little Flat Trail to the first overlook of the Bear Meadows region which cannot be seen from Little Flat Tower.

Move along the edge of Fourth Mountain past a series of overlooks, the white-blazed Fleetfoot Trail, and a trail register. The Mid State Trail here has been moved back from the edge so that hikers will have better footway, but the overlooks can still be reached via short side trails. At 5.0 km bear right on the North Meadows Trail. Shortly the North Meadows Trail turns right and becomes blue-blazed. You can truncate this hike by following it down to Bear Gap Road.

However, the best views are still to come, so bear left and continue on the orange-blazed Mid State Trail, which takes you to the Indian Wells Overlook at 5.6 km. This is one of the great natural overlooks in central Pennsylvania. I had taken this hike dozens of times before I found wild azalea growing along the trail. (I think this shrub should be the state flower instead of the mountain laurel.)

The Indian Wells are the holes that have been dug into the rock pile at this overlook. Some of the wells appear to be very recent but weathering shows others to be older. One possible explanation is that the wells were dug by young braves as part of their coming of age, when they went into the woods and fasted until they started to hallucinate. When members of the Huron tribe, east of Lake Superior, went on these ordeals they dug such wells in the old beach lines of that lake. These pits can be seen in Lake Superior Provincial Park in Ontario.

Beyond the Indian Wells Overlook the Mid State Trail continues across Big Flat, crossing several charcoal flats that make good campsites. Charcoal from Big Flat probably went to Greenwood Furnace many miles to the south. At 6.4 km, turn right on the blue-blazed Keith Spring Trail. Soon you arrive at Keith Spring, named for Professor Keith of the Penn State Chemistry Department, who hiked these hills extensively over half a century ago. Bear right on Bear Gap Road to another overlook cut by the Youth Conservation Corps. From here you can see Tussey Ridge, Kocher Mountain, and Hubler Gap. The towers visible on Tussey Ridge are near PA 26.

Continue downhill on the gated Bear Gap Road, passing first the North Meadows Trail junction and then a piped spring. Beware of mountain bikes that come down this road at warp speed. At the bottom of the hill, turn left onto Laurel Run Road. Just beyond the Sand Spring hunting camp turn right onto the Sand Spring Trail, which is marked with blue rectangles. Cross Laurel Run (you can usually find a log or plank bridge a little way upstream) and bear left. You soon begin climbing the south flank of Tussey or Second Mountain. When you reach the Little Shingletown fire road, jog right before continuing up Tussey Ridge. Note that Little Shingletown Road is marked with blue spots designating its use as a cross-country ski trail, but it is more heavily used by mountain bikes. It provides an easy path back to your car, if you have young children along. This hike continues following the blue rectangles.

At the top of Tussey Ridge, you rejoin the Mid State Trail. You can truncate your hike by turning right for a delightful section of the ridgetop trail back to your car, but 1.2 km to your left is the best view of State College available from anywhere except by air. The path to this overlook is new and rocky but the view is well worth the effort. Beaver Stadium can be seen, but it is too far to see individual cars. On a day when a football game is being played you can see the pattern form in the fields around the stadium as fans park their cars. In the same manner you can watch a crystal grow from a solution although you cannot see the atoms forming it.

To finish your hike, retrace your steps along the ridgetop to the junction with the Sand Spring Trail and then continue on the Mid State Trail to Laurel Run Road, where you left your car. Call Rothrock State Forest at 814-643-2340 for a camping permit.

26

Indian Steps

Distance: 16.0 km (9.9 miles)

Time: 6 hours

Vertical Rise: 340 meters (800 ft)

Highlights: Views, old stone steps

Maps: USGS 7.5' Pine Grove Mills; MSTA Map 202

The Indian Steps seem to be another mystery of Penn's Woods. Nobody today can explain their location (up a mountainside) or say with certainty who built them. According to one legend the steps were built by the Kishacoquillas tribe over 300 years ago, but Paul Wallace, in his book *Indian Paths of Pennsylvania,* does not even mention them. However, their existence prior to 1911 is documented.

The location is unusual because Native American paths usually took easier routes—and an easy route ran across Tussey Mountain less than 5 km away. Called the Standing Stone Path (now called PA 26) and listed by Wallace, it passed through a gap between Leading

and Rudy Ridges just above Monroe Furnace. A Native American on the Standing Stone Path who wanted to use the steps would have had to detour either through Harrys Valley or cross over Leading Ridge near its highest part. Indeed, the best preserved steps of all continue up the northwest flank of Leading Ridge and stop, suspiciously, at the boundary of state forest land on the ridgetop. On Leading Ridge their route parallels a number of old boundary lines, and it seems likely that the Indian Steps were a white man's boundary line in the 19th century.

The hike starts and ends at the parking lot on the top of Tussey Ridge on the west side of PA 26, 2 miles uphill from the intersection of PA 45 and PA 26 in Pine Grove Mills. The ridgetop portions of the hike are on the orange-blazed Mid State Trail (MST). You will want your hiking boots for the notoriously rocky Mid State Trail.

Begin walking south on PA 26 and turn right on the gated road that is the trail at this point. Do not cross PA 26. Continue past a microwave tower and through the woods to an old clear-cut area. Proceed along the trail to the power-line crossing for northwest views of farmland at the foot of Tussey Ridge,

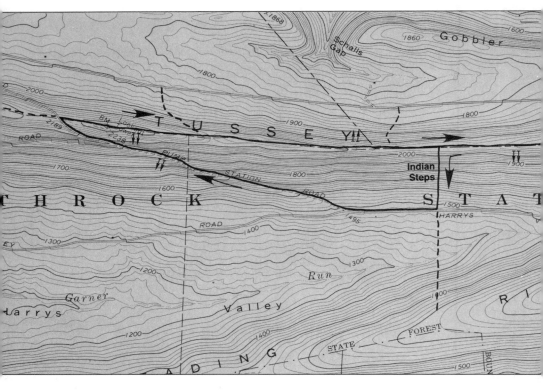

heavily wooded Barrens backed by Bald Eagle Mountain, and the Allegheny Front on the horizon. To the southeast you see upper Stone Valley and Stone Mountain on the horizon. At this point the woods road ends, and the Mid State Trail becomes rough and rocky.

You then pass a trail register and another view to the southeast a bit farther. Continuing, you cross the Campbell Trail at 2.3 km. This trail was a wagon road built across the ridge by a tavern owner named Campbell to deliver thirsty wagoneers to the front door of his tavern and away from the competition in Pine Grove Mills. Proceeding along the ridge, you pass one overlook above Harrys Valley and then three more overlooks.

Finally, at 4.7 km from PA 26, you reach the top of the Indian Steps, marked by a post sign. Turn left and follow the deeply worn and blue-blazed path to the edge of the ridge and then descend. Many steps are missing but near the ridgetop sections are still intact. The Indian Steps Trail continues down to Harrys Valley Road for a steep drop of almost 200 meters. For obscure reasons the trail sign here is labeled Crownover Trail. The Crownover Trail is blue-blazed as part of the Ironstone Loop. Turn right on Harrys Valley Road. On some weekends the traffic may be heavy but at midweek you may not see a single car in the time it takes to cover the 800 meters on the road. Bear right on the next road, the unmarked Pump Station Road. The gentle grade of the road makes for an easy climb back up Tussey Ridge. Toward the ridgetop you pass

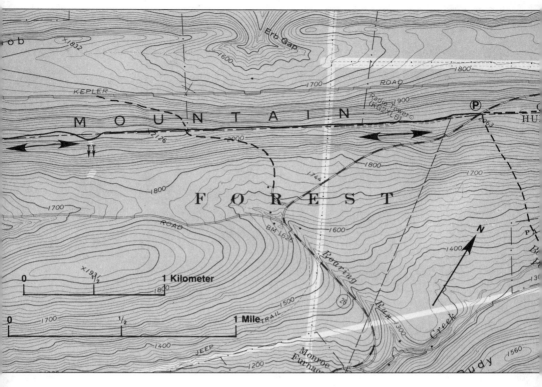

rocky areas with views of Harrys Valley and Leading Ridge and finally connect with Pennsylvania Furnace Road. Continue ahead past several more viewpoints. To the southeast Jacks Mountain rises over the top of Stone Mountain, and Terrace Mountain comes up from the south and ends abruptly. The Juniata River flows just to the north of the mountain's end, and Butler Knob on Jacks Mountain is visible behind Terrace Mountain. One view extends so far south you see Tussey Ridge itself at the loop south of the Little and Frankstown Branches of the Juniata, and at one place you can see west over Tussey Mountain to Canoe Mountain.

At the ridgetop turn sharply right again on the Mid State Trail and proceed along the gated access road past the site of Tussey Fire Tower. The views from the top were truly spectacular.

Beyond the tower site you enter the woods and pass a southeast view of Stone Valley Lake and a blue-blazed side trail to Kepler Road.

You then begin a fairly long pull of 1.4 km to the Schalls Gap Overlook, where a log seat provides a good resting spot. The Indian Steps Trail is 600 meters farther, but only a couple of steps remain on this side of the ridge. For the next 300 meters you follow the old ridgetop trail connecting the Indian Steps Trail on opposite sides of the ridge, and then you retrace your steps on the Mid State Trail to return to PA 26 and your car.

Other hiking opportunities near the Indian Steps include the Jackson Trail on the other side of PA 26 (Hike 18).

27

Cherry Run Gamelands

Distance: 16.0 km (10.0 miles)

Time: 5 hours

Vertical Rise: 290 meters (950 ft)

Highlights: Mountain streams, evergreens

Maps: USGS 7.5' Millheim, Mill Hall; Sportsmen's Recreation Map

Just south of Exit 25 on I-80 at Lamar is a rugged expanse of mountainland known as the Cherry Run Gamelands (State Game Lands (SGL) 295). The Western Pennsylvania Conservancy acquired this land in 1979 by buying every share of stock in the B&R Lumber Company of Johnstown. Thus the Conservancy became the company and was able to transfer this 5200-hectare tract to the Pennsylvania Game Commission at cost. The Conservancy takes a generous view of the boundaries of Western Pennsylvania. This hike is a circuit on unmarked trails in SGL 295.

The Cherry Run Gamelands are a syncline formed by two layers of hard rock, Bald Eagle sandstone from the upper Ordovician and Tuscarora sandstone from the lower Silurian. These layers form four parallel ridges named, from south to north, Sugar Valley, Bear, and Big Mountains. The northernmost ridge doesn't seem to have a name of its own and for the most part it is just a bench on the north flank of Big Mountain.

From PA 64 in Lamar drive south toward Tylersville on SR 2002 for 3.8 miles. A parking lot is on the left just before the bridge over Cherry Run. If you should miss this area there are two alternative areas on the right along the paved road and another on the left at Bear Run. Because of rocks, stream crossings, and wet spots, wear your hiking boots. Despite its length the trail is easy to hike and the climbing is at water level.

To start the hike walk out to SR 2002 and turn left. Walk on the left, facing traffic. It's best to get this road walking over with first. At 800 meters cross Bear Run and turn left to an alternative parking area. Pass a vehicle gate and continue on an old logging road through a green tunnel of hemlocks along Bear Run.

The climb along Bear Run is a gentle one at water level, and affords you many views of this small mountain stream.

Cherry Run

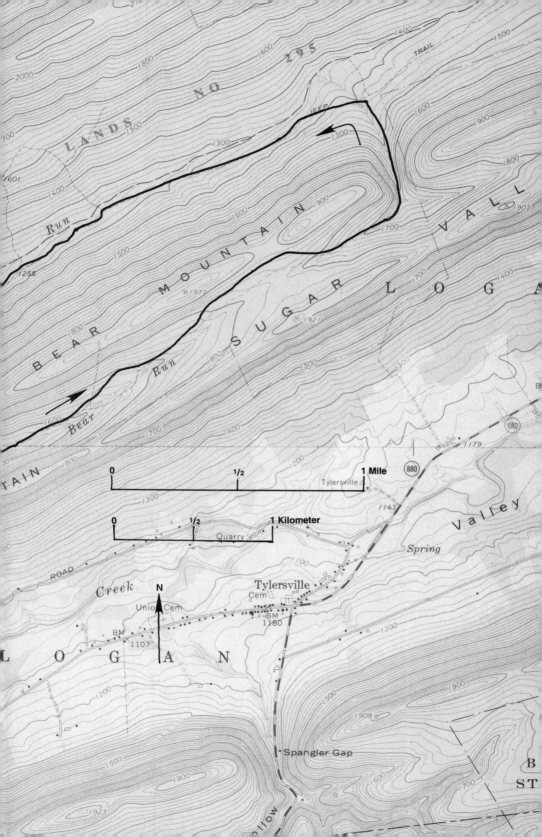

Crossings of Bear Run begin at 2.4 km and all five are without benefit of bridges; at each crossing, though, the stream is a little smaller. As you approach the height-of-land the hemlock gives way to white pine, white oak, and red maple and the trail passes several small meadows. At 6.2 km there is a trail to your right not shown on the USGS map. The height-of-land at 6.8 km is marked by a large clearing that is planted for wildlife, so keep your eyes open. I saw a flock of wild turkeys near here.

Beyond the game food plot continue on a management road that soon starts to descend. The hemlocks take over again and the road swings left into a gap through Bear Mountain.

At the bottom of the hill turn left on Cherry Run Trail where the management road turns right. Then cross a stream that issues from the gap and continue on the old logging road. One of the few landmarks along this section is a junked car at 9.9 km. Presumably it dates back to the lumber company days. Soon Cherry Run itself is visible to your right. Even when you can't see it, you can hear it flowing under the rhododendrons. Native brook trout are alleged to be present in Cherry Run, but the overhanging rhododendrons must make fishing difficult. The entire trail along Cherry Run is bordered with evergreens: hemlocks, white pines, and rhododendrons.

A side trail to your right at 10.6 km crosses Cherry Run. At 13.6 km there is a shack to your left, which must also date from before this area became a gameland. Beyond 15 km a trail and an old road are to your right. Then Cherry Run becomes visible again. Cherry Run Trail is suitable for cross-country skiing as it needs only 15 cm of snow, or less, to be skiable.

At 15.6 km turn right onto a new trail. If you miss this turn you will quickly reach a barrier across Cherry Run Trail, behind a hunting camp, on a small inholding of private land. Cross a footbridge over part of Cherry Run, then bear right to find a second footbridge over the rest of the run. Then turn left and make your way to an old road that is easy to follow. Bear left on the old road. After 100 meters, when you see the old road start to climb ahead, bear left again on a faint old woods road just before crossing a small stream. After another 100 meters you are back at the parking lot on SR 2002.

Additional hiking opportunities can be found in Bald Eagle State Forest east of SGL 295. Drive to the top of Big Mountain on Riansares Road and check out Winter Trail. For those who would like to contribute to the land conservation efforts of the Western Pennsylvania Conservancy, its address is 316 Fourth Avenue, Pittsburgh, PA 15222.

28

Black Moshannon State Park

Distance: 17.2 km (10.7 miles)

Time: 5 hours

Vertical Rise: 60 meters (200 ft)

Highlights: Mountain lake, bogs, and streams

Maps: USGS 7.5' Black Moshannon; park map

Black Moshannon State Park, on the Allegheny Plateau in western Centre County, is one of the few parks in the state with a well-developed system of hiking trails. The longest and most interesting of these trails circles a lake, passes through many stands of evergreens, and runs by an active beaver colony. Almost all the trails are suited for ski touring as the plateau's elevation results in a deep and long-lasting snow cover. Surprisingly, this long trek requires little climbing, and much of the hike runs close to the park's feature, a lake formed by the damming of Black Moshannon Creek north of PA 504.

The park is located in Moshannon State Forest at the junction of PA 504 and the Julian Pike. To reach it, drive east on PA 504 from Philipsburg for 8 miles, or west on PA 504 from Unionville for 11.7 miles, or west on the Julian Pike from Julian for 8.4 miles. Park in the beach lot on the north side of PA 504, in the boat-launching lot on the south side, or across the bridge in the lot near the boat-rental concession.

The hike starts at the junction of PA 504 and the Julian Pike. Begin by crossing the bridge. Keep left along the roadside past the boat-rental area; at the Westside Road/PA 504 junction, bear left up the slope on an unmarked trail. Pass Cabin P6 and turn left. After 100 meters turn left again, soon reaching a junction with the white-blazed Seneca Trail. Turn right on the Seneca Trail and follow it to where it joins the Hayroad Trail. Continue on; at the junction with Indian Trail, turn left, and follow Indian Trail through a planting of jack pine and Norway spruce as far as the Moss Hanna Trail.

The Moss Hanna Trail, which you follow for the next 12.5 km, is marked with orange blazes that vary in size and shape. Double blazes are used to mark turns. Along the first stretch the Moss Hanna

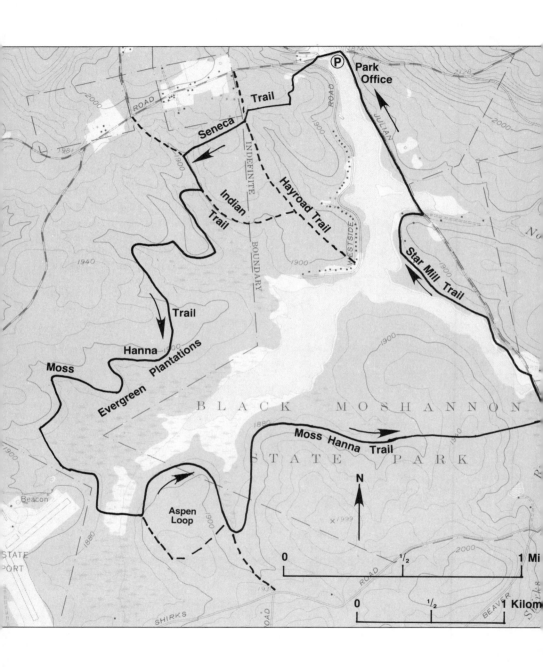

Moss Hanna Trail in pine plantation

Trail crosses the head of a long, swampy arm of the lake, then on higher ground passes several old beaver dams. Although the trail here is scarcely 1 km from an access road to the local airport, it feels remote as it winds through open woods and dense stands of red pine and Norway spruce, traversing both high ground and the lake's marshy extensions. At 6.0 km the trail follows a relocation through the woods to avoid some wet spots.

Before reaching the airport fence, the trail turns left on a boardwalk through an alder swamp. This relocation affords you an opportunity to inspect the bog close up. At the far end the Moss Hanna Trail turns left again in sight of the fence enclosing Mid-State Airport. (The fence and cattle gate on the access road are supposed to keep deer off the runways.) The trail veers from the fence, circles the end of a runway, and passes between the approach lights. You can see Rattlesnake Mountain down the approach light swath.

You now leave the woods and take another boardwalk across a broad, marshy area, in the midst of which you cross Black Moshannon Creek on a new bridge. In the late summer the creek may be almost dry, but in midwinter it flows deep and clear and rarely freezes. Once across the bridge you climb into the woods, passing the blue-blazed Aspen Trail on your right. Bear left, then right, and follow a faint woods road across higher ground to another marshy indenture of the lake.

Here the trail bears right and the woods road becomes clearer. You cross what seems to be a small strip mine and can see pulverized coal on the path and small piles of coal in the brush. Nobody seems to know who operated this mine or when, but the fact is the whole park sits on a subsurface coal seam. The state does not own the mineral rights and one would guess the owners will someday insist on removing their coal. The lake already contains a quantity of acid and such activity would increase its acidity and destroy its ability to support any form of aquatic life.

You next pass the other end of the Aspen Trail and then turn left off the woods road. (Ahead the woods road leads out to Shirks Road.) Cross a small stream and round the head of the bay. Bear left and pass a large spring. Soon you see old beaver dams on your left, an active dam farther ahead, and a classic beaver lodge in the pond. Many trees in this area have been felled by the beavers.

The trail then bears east, gradually draws away from the lake, passes through a dense stand of hemlocks, and crosses higher ground before entering another pine plantation. You take a corduroy trail through the marsh along Shirks Run, and cross the run on a bridge to reach Julian Pike.

Turn left and walk single file on the left side of the pike, facing traffic. After crossing Smays Run, take a sharp left onto the unblazed Star Mill Trail and follow it along the lake edge. After 1 km bear left on the road at the cottage and return to Julian Pike. Turn left and cross North Run. Once across, walk on the grass to the left of the road. After you pass the road to the group camping area, bear left and finish your hike by traversing the extended picnic area between the road and the lake. You are now at the boat-launching area and close to your car.

Additional hiking opportunities can be found on Rock Run Trail (Hike 21) near Black Moshannon State Park.

NORTH DISTRICT

29

Pitch Pine Loop

Distance: 4 km (2.5 miles)	
Time: 1¼ hours	
Vertical Rise: 20 meters (60 ft)	
Highlights: Views	
Maps: USGS 7.5' Jersey Mills, Glen Union	

Pitch Pine Loop is one of many trails blazed primarily for ski touring in recent years. Tiadaghton State Forest, in which this hike is located, has probably undergone the most activity of all 20 state forest districts regarding the clearing and marking of trails for hiking and ski touring. *Tiadaghton* is a Native American word meaning "river of pines," and most of Pine Creek Gorge is located in this state forest. Tioga State Forest to the north contains the balance.

PA 44, the only access to this hike, follows much of the early 19th-century Jersey Shore–to–Coudersport Turnpike. This pike was famous for the long distance it traversed through a wilderness devoid of human settlement. Even to-

day, over 160 years later, PA 44 is virtually bereft of permanent human inhabitants from Haneyville to Sweden Valley. Most of the buildings you see along the way are hunting camps, and they are usually occupied only the night before deer season opens.

Walking shoes are fine for this short hike with good footway. The trailhead is on the east side of PA 44, 2.6 miles north of the junction with PA 664 in Haneyville. Park on the small hard-surfaced area and begin hiking on the blue-blazed trail close by. Bear left, heading slowly away from the highway, and pass behind a hunting camp. (If you don't pass in back of this camp you are following blazes in the wrong direction.) About 500 meters from the start a faint unblazed trail diverges left down a draw into the Miller Run Natural Area. You stay to the right, up on the plateau, and pass through a stand of scrub oaks and the pitch pines for which the trail is named. Both these trees grow in poor, dry, sandy soil. The pitch pine has a superficial resemblance to the red pine on the nearby Baldwin Point hike (Hike 38). Here in Penn's Woods, pitch pines become real forest trees. Before the Revolution, tar and turpentine were made from them, and their rot-resistant wood

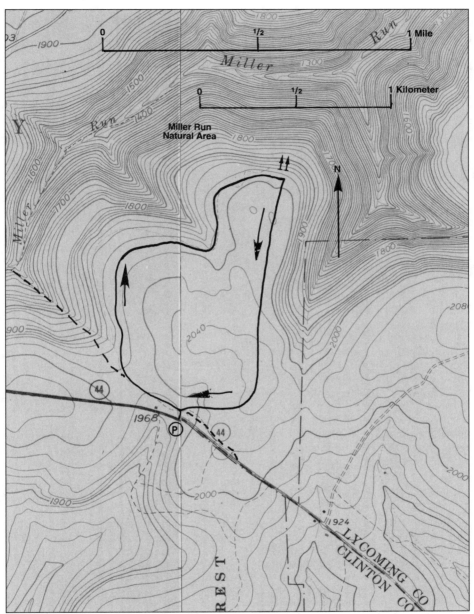

was used in making waterwheels. Look for the characteristic tufts of needles that emerge on miniature branches from the pitch pine's trunk. These tufts help you to distinguish it from red pine, which it otherwise resembles. Pitch pines are the most fire-resistant of any tree in Penn's Woods.

Brown thrasher's nest

At 2.3 km from the start you reach an overlook with an extensive vista over the 1600-hectare Miller Run Natural Area. The farthest hillsides are on the east side of Pine Creek.

The trail back to the parking area takes off just behind this view. It is not as wide as the old road you followed up, and it twists and turns more through the woods.

The last stretch goes by all too fast, but just 100 meters from the end you encounter one more point of interest when you pass through a small stand of larch. These trees appear to be the only survivors of 10,900 seedlings of larch, red pine, and pitch pine planted here on April 23, 1941 by the Civilian Conservation Corps. The planting report noted heavy root competition, sterile soil (the area burned in 1931), and severe deer damage as unfavorable conditions. The report also noted that liberation from scrub oak competition would be needed in 2 or 3 years. By then the Civilian Conservation Corps was fighting World War II and you see the results about you: an abundance of scrub oak. Larch is a deciduous conifer; its needles turn a smoky gold color before they are shed in the fall.

You now walk the short distance back to the highway and your car.

30

Gillespie Point

Distance: 6.1 km (3.8 miles)

Time: 2¾ hours

Vertical Rise: 275 meters (900 ft)

Highlights: Views

Maps: USGS 7.5' Cedar Run, Morris

High above the village of Blackwell at the confluence of Pine and Babb Creeks is a hill called Gillespie Point. It is known locally as Pennsylvania's Matterhorn. The Bureau of Forestry has cut and blazed a trail to the summit of this hill and sites have been cleared to provide views. The pyramidal shape of Gillespie Point is unusual among mountains in the Allegheny Plateau, and you can see the hill's distinctive pointed outline from as far down Pine Creek as Gas Line Ridge below State Run.

Blackwell marks the southern end of Pine Creek's narrow valley, referred to as the Grand Canyon of Pennsylvania. However, Pine Creek Gorge continues all the way down to the west branch of the Susquehanna near the town of Jersey Shore. Walking shoes are fine for this hike.

The trailhead is at the junction of PA 414 and Big Run Road in the village of Blackwell. No real parking area exists so park as best you can along the sides of Big Run Road or PA 414. Or you could park in the large lot at the take-out point just below the PA 414 bridge and walk through Blackwell on the highway to Big Run Road.

You begin the blue-blazed trail about 100 meters from the highway at the bend in Big Run Road, following an old wagon road that slabs up the steep side of the gorge. The grade is relentless so move slowly. (You can climb faster this way than if you surge ahead and stop to catch your breath.)

Partway up you pass a walled spring and an extensive stand of white birch. At 900 meters the old wagon road tops out at the edge of the canyon and you turn sharply left to continue up the ridgeline. After another 700 meters you enter the clearing around the rock outcrops at the summit. It's an old story in Penn's Woods that you can't see the forest for the trees. If these vistas had not been cut you would have no views during the months the trees were in leaf.

As you pause for breath you look out

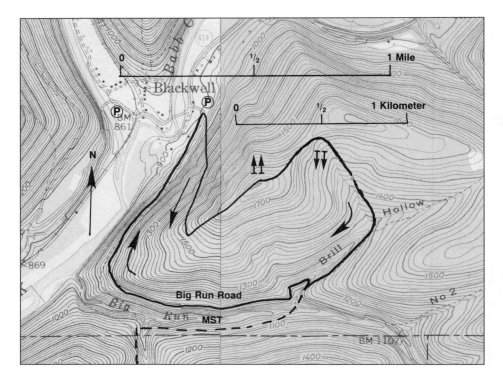

over a few buildings in Blackwell and the road bridge over Pine Creek. You can't see very far up the creek but you do see an expanse of it downstream to the southwest. The Grand Canyon of Pennsylvania, from Ansonia to Blackwell, is a favorite float trip for rafts and canoes. Notice the take-out point just below the bridge. Try to imagine what Pine Creek looked like at the peak of the last continental ice sheet. The ice advanced approximately to the New York State line, and Pine Creek carried all the meltwater from a vast stretch of the ice front. No wonder its valley looks a bit oversized for the modest stream of today! If you walk a few steps through the trees you come to another overlook, with a vista up Babb

Creek. You can see a few buildings in Morris far up the valley.

At this point you can truncate your hike by returning the way you came; or you can continue on the circuit hike. To do so follow the orange Mid State Trail (MST) blazes down the ridgeline. At 2.0 km there is a view south over Big Run Valley to Oregon Hill. Just beyond, turn right in the saddle and descend in a no-cut corridor between clear-cuts, crossing a logging road. Cross a stream and then bear right on Brill Hollow Trail. Turn right on Big Run Road at 3.5 km and follow it back to the outskirts of Blackwell and your car.

Other hiking opportunities near Blackwell include Bohen Run Falls (Hike 36) and the West Rim Trail (Hike 39).

31

Forrest H. Dutlinger Natural Area

Distance: 6.8 km (4.2 miles)	
Time: 2½ hours	
Vertical Rise: 275 meters (900 ft)	
Highlights: Old-growth timber	
Maps: USGS 7.5' Hammersley Fork, Tamarack	

At the head of Beech Bottom Hollow on the Hammersley Fork is a small stand of old-growth hemlock, the heart of the 600-hectare Forrest H. Dutlinger Natural Area. This stand appears to have been on the border between two logging operations, one headed by a man named Munson and the other headed by the Goodyear brothers. Like similar boundaries, it was not well delineated, and to avoid paying triple damages for boundary violation the operators never cut these trees. The trees are a monument to poor surveying, just like many other small tracts of virgin timber throughout Penn's Woods.

However, this stand is probably not real virgin timber. The white pine was removed, leaving only stumps and room for hardwoods to grow. Pennsylvania loggers would go a long way for white pine, and it may have been cut before the logging railway era, when the boundary dispute arose.

Forrest H. Dutlinger, for whom the natural area is named, served the Department of Forests for 50 years after his graduation from the Pennsylvania State Forest Academy at Mount Alto in 1908. He was the first professional forester assigned to what is now Sproul State Forest, where he implemented progressive forestry practices. He also served as District Forester in Rothrock State Forest.

The trailhead is just off PA 144 between the villages of Cross Fork and Hammersley Fork. Over the years the latter village has moved downstream and is now centered about Trout Run. Drive northeast on PA 144 for 1.6 miles from the junction with Kettle Creek Road and then bear left on the old road for 0.1 mile. Turn left onto a gravel road immediately after crossing the old bridge over Hammersley Fork; in 0.6 mile more you are at the edge of state forest lands. Park somewhere in the next 0.1 mile, before you reach the ford

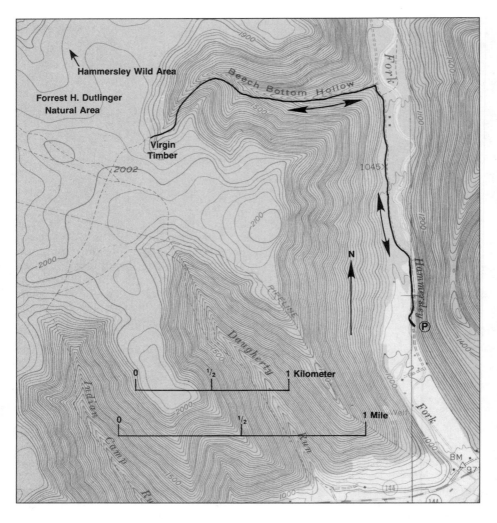

across Hammersley Fork. The road is closed to all but four-wheel-drive vehicles at this point. Ordinary walking shoes are fine for this hike.

The footbridge about 100 meters upstream has been replaced by a cable bridge, which may be used to cross Hammersley Fork. I found this bridge had such alarming vibrations that I took off my boots and forded the stream. On the far side turn right on the jeep road along the edge of the stream and eventually swing left toward the valley's west side. The careful observer should see the remains of old hunting camps and railroad grades along the stream valley's bottom.

At 1.7 km you reach the junction with Beech Bottom Trail at the mouth of Beech Bottom Run. This is the first trail you reach by the Hammersley Fork beyond a stone chimney. There is usually a sign at this junction. Turn left and start the long but steady climb up Beech Bottom Hollow. This trail is probably an old log slide. You stick close to the run at first but gradually climb above it. A spring is just to the left of the trail at 3.0 km.

You reach the hemlock at 3.4 km, at just about the top of the hollow. A trail register stands to the left. This is the only remaining tract of Pennsylvania's Black Forest, which stretched east of here to Pine Creek and also covered most of Potter County. With the exhaustion of white pine late in the 19th century, the price of hemlock rose sharply. The vast stands of hemlock lasted so short a time after the price increase that in only 3 decades they were gone. Entire towns and railroad networks were built to exploit the hemlock, and when it was gone, they too vanished. But this is what it was like—hemlocks so thick and large that sunlight rarely reached the ground even at midday.

When you have seen enough, retrace your steps to your car.

32

Haystacks

Distance: 7.1 km (4.4 miles)	
Time: 2¾ hours	
Vertical Rise: 105 meters (350 ft)	
Highlights: Rapids, waterfall	
Maps: USGS 7.5' Laporte; Loyalsock Trail Map 3	

At its easternmost end the Loyalsock Trail closely parallels its namesake creek. Along this section of the creek there are many rapids, the largest of which is called the Haystacks. The Haystacks is formed by a resistant layer of rock known as the Burgoon or Pocono sandstone. The Burgoon is lower Mississippian in age and consists of river deposits laid down on a coastal plain at the end of the Catskill Delta formation. It is a prominent ridge-former in the eastern and central Allegheny Plateau, and for long sections it also forms the edge of the Allegheny Plateau itself.

The trailhead is on US 220 north of Laporte in Sullivan County just 3.0 miles north of the PA 154 junction. Park on the west side of the highway near a small sign for the Loyalsock Trail (LT). Due to rocks, stream crossings, and other wet spots you will want your boots on this hike.

Dodge around the gate and start your hike on the old grade of the Williamsport and North Bend Railroad. The Williamsport and North Bend was a standard-gauge railroad that served a number of sawmills, some chemical plants, and a coal mine before it was abandoned in 1937. The main Loyalsock Trail is marked with red and yellow paint blazes of superior quality. Pass under a power line and shortly turn right on Red-X Trail 11. This trail is marked with tin can lids painted yellow with a red X. Then cross a stream on rocks at the brink of Dutchman Falls. This part of the Loyalsock Trail is behind the terminal moraine of the last ice age, so waterfalls are fairly common. You will have to climb down along the falls to get a good look.

Back on the Red-X Trail descend steeply to Loyalsock Creek and proceed downstream for about 300 meters. Then climb steeply, reaching the main trail at 1.0 km. Bear right on an old road grade and descend. Proceed downstream, passing a woods road to the left at 3.0 km. Soon you come to rapids in the creek. Ignore another red-X trail at 3.2 km and

Dutchman Falls

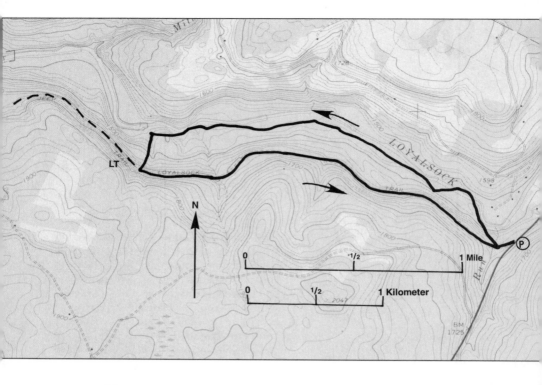

cross a side stream. Next the trail skirts the edge of the creek, with low cliffs to your left and more rapids to your right. At 3.5 km you reach the best view of the Haystacks. The Burgoon sandstone has eroded into rounded shapes, and in low water the creek pursues tortuous paths between them. In spring's high water, the creek may go right over the rocks to produce spectacular waves.

Beyond the Haystacks bear left and start to climb back to the Williamsport and North Bend Railroad grade. At 3.7 km you pass a trail register. Please register so the Alpine Club of Williamsport will have a reliable idea of usage on this trail it maintains. Continue climbing to the railroad grade, and turn left on Red-X Trail 10. There is a small waterfall at this point; you pass another at 4.4 km. In about 100 meters ignore a red-X trail that returns to the Haystacks. Proceed along the railroad grade to a junction with the Loyalsock main trail at 6.2 km. Continue east on the Loyalsock Trail to a junction with Red-X Trail 11. Then retrace the few steps to your car on US 220.

Other hikes that contain lots of water-falls can be found at Ricketts Glen State Park.

33

Smiths Knob

Distance: 9.1 km (5.7 miles)

Time: 4½ hours

Vertical Rise: 356 meters (1170 ft)

Highlights: Views and mountain stream

Maps: USGS 7.5' Huntersville; Loyalsock Trail Map 1

This circuit hike was suggested by hikers in the Williamsport area. It uses part of the Loyalsock Trail (LT), which is maintained by the Alpine Club of Williamsport.

To reach the trailhead, drive north on PA 87 for 9.3 miles from I-180 (US 220) in Montoursville, passing the trailhead for the Loyalsock Trail (Hike 34). Turn right on Little Bear Creek Road and follow it for 0.8 mile to the ranger station. There is ample parking between the road and Little Bear Creek. You will want your hiking boots for this hike.

Turn your steps back down the road, passing the bridge across Little Bear Creek, where you pick up the Loyalsock Trail. In another 100 meters turn right onto the trail, which soon begins a steep

climb up the side of Laurel Ridge. After the slope eases off, you reach the lower edge of the laurel belt and the footway becomes more rocky.

There are three kinds of side trails along the Loyalsock Trail: white, blue, and red. White side trails are not cleared and they may or may not return to the Loyalsock Trail. Blue side trails do not return to the Loyalsock Trail but are cleared. Red side trails return to the Loyalsock Trail and are also cleared. All these side trails are marked by tin can lids of the appropriate color nailed to trees. The main trail has recently been re-marked by the best paint blazes I've ever seen. The tree bark has been carefully scraped, and three coats of yellow paint have been skillfully applied. A red band was then applied to the middle of the blaze. Turns are indicated by yellow arrows that emerge from the top of the blaze, then bend in the appropriate direction. The old tin can lids have been left on during the changeover period, but they will be retained in a reduced capacity after 1995.

At 1.3 km you reach a junction with White Trail 1, a marked bushwhack that leads to PA 87. This point is named "Lookout Rocks" and has recently been cleared to provide a view over the valley

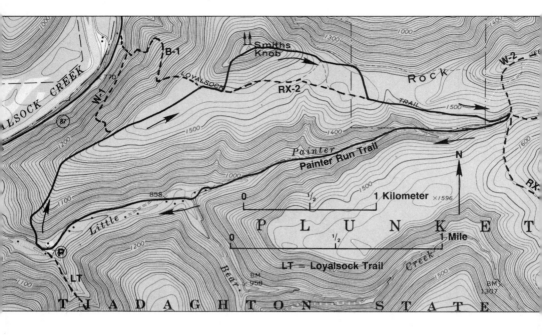

of Loyalsock Creek. Soon after is a second recently cleared view.

Stay on the Loyalsock Trail, which turns right on an old woods road at 2.3 km. At this junction the road to the left is Blue Trail 1, which also leads to PA 87. (According to the USGS map, this is a former route of the Loyalsock.)

Soon, you turn left and resume climbing. (Ahead the old woods road becomes Red-X Trail 2, which returns to the Loyalsock Trail beyond Smiths Knob.) Continue on the main Loyalsock Trail, which climbs steeply to the top of Smiths Knob passing yet another overlook—this one to the south.

There is still another fine overlook on the far side of Smiths Knob. Be careful as you approach the edge; these are real cliffs, a rarity in Penn's Woods and very dangerous. Below you is the Loyalsock valley and PA 87. During the height of the last ice age, the edge of the continental ice sheet was probably visible from this

point. At that time Loyalsock Creek must have been swollen with enormous floods caused by the melting ice front. In this rugged terrain, however, the terminal moraine of the continental ice sheet is not impressive. This view from Smiths Knob is only one of many great views along the Loyalsock Trail.

To continue your hike descend steeply from Smiths Knob and follow the edge of Rock Ridge on a woods road. At 3.5 km there is a view left downstream along Loyalsock Creek. About 100 meters farther, bear left where the woods road swings south. Soon the Loyalsock Trail also swings south across Rock Ridge to avoid an indentation of private land, and at 4.1 km Red-X Trail 2 comes in on your right as promised. At 4.3 km you cross a woods road and shortly beyond you bear right and follow the same old road. At 5.0 km bear right again on the Loyalsock Trail and shortly you come to Painter Run. *Painter* probably refers to Panther

View from Smiths Knob

or Mountain Lion. A mountain lion may have been killed in this valley before the species was exterminated in the 19th century. Today there is some evidence, in the form of footprints and occasional sightings, that *Felis concolor* has returned to Penn's Woods. If this is the case, these predators are keeping a low profile, but we can certainly spare a few deer to keep them well fed.

Here you leave the marked Loyalsock Trail and turn downstream along Painter Run. There is trail almost all of the way along Painter Run, and if you start out on its right side there are only three crossings. Take time to admire the wildflowers. At the time of one of my visits, red trillium were in bloom, but at any time Painter Run is a beautiful mountain stream.

At 7.5 km cross Painter Run for the last time and soon bear to the left of a hunting camp. Shortly beyond, turn right onto Little Bear Creek Road for the 1.2-km walk back to your car at the ranger station.

This hike could be combined with Hike 34 (Loyalsock Trail) to form a 19-km, 9-hour bootbuster. An obvious car shuttle along the Little Bear Creek Road would save you about 3 km and is recommended if you want to combine these two hikes. You could also extend this hike by taking White Trail 2, which leaves the Loyalsock Trail at the first crossing of Painter Run and returns to the Loyalsock Trail near the next crossing. White Trail 2 leads to spectacular overlooks along Rock Ridge.

A map and guide set to the Loyalsock Trail is available from the Alpine Club of Williamsport. Write the club at PO Box 501, Williamsport, PA 17703 for the current price. For a camping permit call Tiadaghton State Forest at 717-327-3450.

34

Loyalsock Trail

Distance: 10.1 km (6.3 miles)

Time: 4½ hours

Vertical Rise: 355 meters (1165 ft)

Highlights: Views

Maps: USGS 7.5' Montoursville North, Huntersville; Loyalsock Trail Map 1

This rugged hike is on one of the oldest maintained trails in central Pennsylvania. The Loyalsock Trail (LT) was first marked in 1953 and 10 years later was extended and extensively relocated. It parallels Loyalsock Creek, which cuts a deep canyon into the Allegheny Plateau. The Loyalsock Trail has recently been reblazed with red and yellow paint blazes of superior quality. Turns are indicated by yellow arrows that emerge from the top of the blaze and bend in the appropriate direction. The old tin can lids that previously marked the trail will be removed in 1995.

To reach the trailhead, drive north 8.8 miles on PA 87 from the junction with I-180 (US 220) near Montoursville. Sev-

eral parking spaces are found on the east side of the highway. Wear your hiking boots on this outing.

You immediately begin climbing away from the road and soon bear right on an old road for about 250 meters. Then turn left and make a steep climb through a break in the cliffs. Above the cliffs the climb eases off. Hikers have worn a footway into the hillside here, but higher up the rocks become larger and you must watch the markers carefully.

At 1 km you pass a large sandstone boulder named Sock Rock; in another 200 meters you are at the top. Laurel Flat, the plateau, is covered with mountain laurel, usually in full bloom about mid-June.

At 2.5 km you reach a junction of woods roads. The road to the left is marked with a red X and rejoins the Loyalsock Trail near the head of Pete's Hollow. Continue on the other road across two small streams. Follow the trail left at a fork, and left again when it leaves the road. You climb over more rocks and arrive on the Allegheny Front at 3.6 km.

Despite the prominence of the Allegheny Front in Pennsylvania geography, few places offer a walk along this dividing line. This is one, and as you trek the next 2 km the ridge-and-valley region lies on your right and the Allegheny Pla-

teau on your left. Succeeding overlooks offer views of North White Deer Ridge, with the West Branch of the Susquehanna just east of where the ridge fades. Each view is better than the last; the series culminates in an open, spectacular view at Hill 1912. The twin plumes of steam you see are from the Berwick Nuclear Power Plant.

If you hike in June you may witness the antics of a hen grouse. While her chicks fly or scurry in one direction, she displays

View from Allegheny Front

her tail feathers and runs across the trail, cheeping piteously, with one wing dragging as if broken. You are expected to fall for this age-old ruse and follow her into the woods. The "broken wing" mends miraculously, and the hen takes flight to circle around and gather her brood.

At 5.6 km turn right on a woods road and pass the red-X trail on your left. Turn left at the next junction and at 6 km turn left again to head down Pete's Hollow. A short way along a clear-cut on your right offers a view of Smiths Knob across Little Bear Creek Valley. The trail down Pete's Hollow is rough and rocky, so move carefully. Toward the bottom you pick up an old road grade called Peter's Path, pass a trail register at 7.9 km, cross Little Bear Creek, and then turn left on the forest road. In 100 meters the Loyalsock Trail turns right and starts its climb over Smiths Knob (Hike 33), but you continue ahead and at 9.3 km turn left on PA 87 for the short walk back to your car.

This hike may be combined with Hike 33, over Smiths Knob, to form a 19-km, 9-hour bootbuster. An obvious car shuttle along Little Bear Creek Road would save you about 3 km and is recommended if you combine these hikes.

A map and guide set to the Loyalsock Trail is available from the Alpine Club of Williamsport. Write the club at PO Box 501, Williamsport, PA 17703 for the current price. For a camping permit call Tiadaghton State Forest at 717-327-3450.

35

Little Pine State Park

Distance: 10.4 km (6.5 miles)

Time: 5 hours

Vertical Rise: 630 meters (2060 ft)

Highlights: Views, old stone quarries, flood control dam

Maps: USGS 7.5' Waterville, Jersey Mills, English Center; MSTA Map 209; park map

Little Pine State Park is one of the gems of Pine Creek country. From the family camping area set in a grove of white pines to the swimming beach and picnic areas, it affords a special sanctuary from the pressures of the outside world. The park is set in Tiadaghton State Forest where a series of short and long trails have been developed. In addition, the Mid State and Tiadaghton Trails pass through the park. With the destruction of the footbridge at the far end of the reservoir this has become a car shuttle hike. The last log drive in Pennsylvania was made on Little Pine Creek in 1909.

Little Pine State Park is located on SR 4001 between PA 44 at Waterville and PA 287 at English Center. From Waterville drive 5.6 miles upstream, passing the park headquarters and picnic area, to a small parking area on the creek side of the road opposite Panther Run Trail. Leave one car here. Turn back, drive 2.3 miles, and turn into the campground entrance; you can park in the visitor and fisherman parking lot before you reach the contact station. You will want your hiking boots for this expedition in Penn's Woods.

Walk back up the entrance road and cross the highway. The pink-blazed Spike Buck Hollow Trail starts on the far side of the road. This is the route followed by the Mid State Trail (MST) through the park. An elaborate color code has been worked out for the trails at Little Pine.

The Spike Buck switchbacks up the steep slope, where dogwoods grow, and then turns right on an old road grade that continues to climb to a stone quarry. These quarries are common along Pine Creek, and much of Williamsport must have been built or paved with their output. Only rather thin-bedded sandstone seems to have been of interest. There is a view across Boone Run here, and a bit farther on there is another quarry and another view. The trail

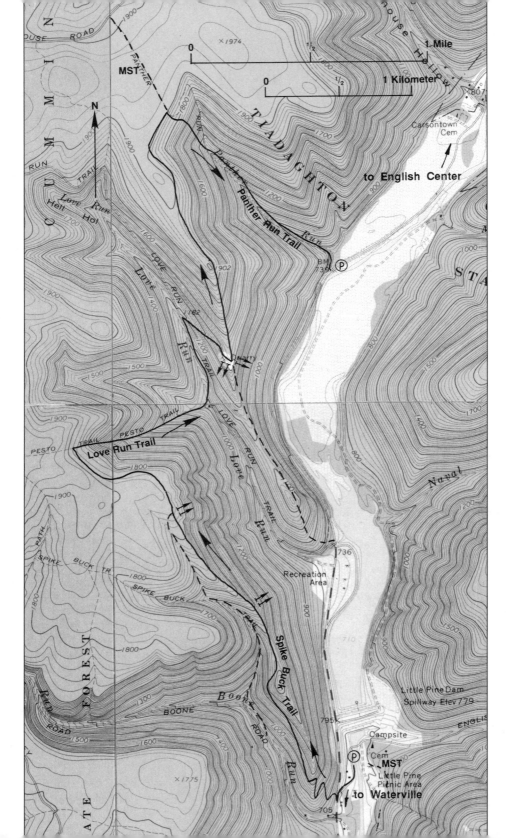

to English Center

to Waterville

1 Mile

1 Kilometer

MST

Panther Run Trail

Love Run Trail

PESTO

Spike Buck Trail

Recreation Area

Little Pine Dam
Spillway Elev 779

Campsite

Little Pine
Picnic Area

MST

Carsontown Cem

Naval

FOREST

BOONE

ROAD

×1974

×1775

N

then switchbacks to the ridgetop, which is knife-edged in places.

At 1.9 km you reach a view across Little Pine Creek from some big rocks. The slope is so steep here that you look down on the far side of the lake impounded behind the flood control dam. The Spike Buck Trail turns left at 2.6 km and loops back to Boone Road. (This is an opportunity to shorten this hike.) Note the lightning scar on a chestnut oak at this junction. There is also a view up Little Pine Creek.

Continue ahead on the green-blazed Love Run Trail which skirts the edge of the plateau. At 3.7 km you pass a spring to the left and at 4.1 km you follow the green blazes right, descending on the Pesto Trail. Hemlock Spring emerges from under a giant hemlock at 4.4 km. At 5.2 km you cross a footbridge behind a hunting camp and then bear left up Love Run Road. (You could also truncate this hike by turning right on this road.) Turn right at 6.0 km and climb an old grade that leads to another stone quarry. The green-blazed Love Run Trail turns right here and follows this ridge back to the park. There are good views of Little Pine Creek and Love Run Valley just a few meters to the right. After taking in the view, you continue left on the yellow-blazed Panther Run Trail, which completes the climb back to the plateau.

At 8.5 km you reach another trail junction. The orange-blazed Mid State Trail goes left to Schoolhouse Road and Bark Cabin Natural Area; but you turn right to stay on the yellow-blazed Panther Run Trail. Soon there is a view to the left and then the trail really starts to descend. Panther Run is steep and has plenty of waterfalls and cascades. At 10.0 km you bear right, away from the run, and then switchback down a very steep bank. Soon you emerge on the paved road across from your car.

If you want to hike more at Little Pine State Park you can follow the Mid State Trail south to Dam Run Road, or follow it north across Schoolhouse and Hackett Roads to the Bark Cabin Natural Area.

Mid State Trail map and guide sets can be mail-ordered from Mid State Trail Association, PO Box 167, Boalsburg, PA 16827.

36

Bohen Run Falls

Distance: 11.5 km (7.1 miles)

Time: 4½ hours

Vertical Rise: 365 meters (1200 ft)

Highlights: Waterfalls, mountain stream, view

Map: USGS 7.5' Cedar Run; West Rim Trail map

To many outdoorspeople, Pine Creek Gorge is the best part of Penn's Woods. This hike uses parts of the Mid State and West Rim Trails, as well as an unmarked trail, to take you past waterfalls on Bohen and Jerry Runs and a view of Pine Creek Gorge.

During the ice ages, when Pine Creek carried meltwater from the continental ice sheet, its valley eroded faster than its side streams. This differential erosion produced waterfalls on many of the side streams, as well as the steep walls and cliffs of Pine Creek Gorge.

The trailhead for this hike is the boater's access area at Blackwell, 5.3 miles west on PA 414 from the junction

with PA 287 in Morris. The parking lot is next to the new PA 414 bridge over Penns Creek. There are pit toilets and a water pump at this area. You'll want your boots for this hike as there are plenty of rocks and wet spots. When there is snow or ice on the ground, do not attempt this hike without instep crampons.

Start your hike by walking across the PA 414 bridge. At the far end, climb over the guardrail and turn right onto the orange-blazed Mid State Trail (MST). Follow the old road to the site of the old bridge, and continue on the trail. This section is cut into the side of the steep slope. Take care not to step off the trail. This section was cut by the Trail Care Team of the Keystone Trails Association on June 6, 1987. The turnout of 28 trail workers for that event is a record that has been tied only once and never exceeded. Soon the trail climbs through a break in the cliff and then levels off farther up the slope.

At 0.9 km bear left on an old grade and cross a dry watercourse. From a rock at 1.3 km there are leaves-off views of Pine Creek. Continue along the slope to the falls of Jerry Run. These falls are of the buttermilk type in that the flow spreads out over the face of the rock. The best view is from a ledge to the right of

the trail. Be careful—there is quite a drop to the stream below and the rock is cracked near the edges.

Cross Jerry Run and continue down another grade to a junction with a blue-blazed side trail at 2.0 km that leads to several campsites along Pine Creek.

Bear left on an old road at this point. Next, you pass above Bohen Run Falls. The falls are best seen by following the blue-blazed side trail to the right. Back on the Mid State, continue up Bohen

Run, which has many smaller falls and riffles, to a signed junction with the West Rim Trail. Turn sharply left on the orange-blazed West Rim Trail. Do not cross Bohen Run or continue upstream on yet another blazed trail.

Climb slowly up the side of the canyon. At 5.1 km there is a view south over Jerry Run, Pine Creek, Blackwell, and Gillespie Point. Oregon Hill forms the southern horizon. There are usually a few logs here, and it makes a great lunch stop.

Moving on along the edge of Pine Creek Gorge, the trail bears right near a hunting camp. Watch the blazes carefully here as the trail is poorly defined. At 6.3 km cross West Rim Road, which offers you your only option to truncate this hike, by following the road left down to PA 414. In midweek there is very little traffic on this state forest road.

Continue ahead on a gated jeep road and pass a dynamite shed that is no longer used. (No need to tiptoe.) Just beyond, the trail takes you along the edge of a clear-cut with a white pine plantation on your right. At 6.8 km turn left on an unmarked jeep road that passes through a patch of sweet fern growing in the clear-cut. (If you miss this unmarked turn, continue down the West Rim Trail to PA 414, where you turn left on the highway to return to Blackwell, adding about 1.6 km to your hike.)

Soon you reenter the woods. Follow the jeep road carefully as it is much less traveled here. Soon it becomes an honest trail as it swings left toward the edge of Pine Creek Gorge. At 8.5 km turn right at the edge of the gorge and follow the trail downhill. It appears that this trail is a former route of West Rim Road but with a steeper grade than the present one. There are some leaves-off views across the gorge. At 9.6 km you reach the white-blazed boundary of state forest land. If the private land ahead is posted, turn left along the white blazes and follow them downhill to West Rim Road, visible below, where you turn right. If the private land is not posted, continue down the old grade.

At 9.9 km bear right on West Rim Road and follow it around the corner to PA 414. The abandoned Conrail grade is slated to become a hike-bike trail. If this has taken place by the time of your visit, bear left on the road, then find a way down the steep bank and turn left. Follow the railroad grade on its own bridge over Pine Creek and then make your way to the parking lot. Otherwise, turn left on PA 414 and follow it back to the highway bridge over Pine Creek and the parking lot just beyond.

Nearby hiking opportunities are found at Gillespie Point (Hike 30) and the West Rim Trail (Hike 39).

A map of the West Rim Trail can be obtained from Tioga State Forest, Box 94, Route 287S, Wellsboro, PA 16901. Call 717-724-2868 for a camping permit.

37

Splash Dam Hollow

Distance: 12.5 km (7.8 miles)

Time: 4 hours

Vertical Rise: 290 meters (950 ft)

Highlights: Beaver dams

Maps: USGS 7.5' Brookland, Cherry Springs; Susquehannock Trail Map 1

The Susquehannock Trail System (STS) opened for hiking in 1969. Most of this giant loop trail lies in Potter County, but it strays over the line into Clinton County in three or four places. The STS passes through Patterson Picnic Area and Ole Bull State Park, and skirts Prouty Picnic Area, Lyman Run, and Cherry Springs and Denton Hill State Parks. It also traverses the Hammersley Wild Area. Part of this circuit hike follows an unblazed, little-used trail for which you may need your compass.

The trailhead is at the district office for Susquehannock State Forest, located on the south side of US 6 at the top of the hill between Denton Hill State Park and Sweden Valley. Park along the road between the office building and the equipment garage. There are public rest rooms on the side of the garage. Except for some wet spots and a stream crossing, you can get by with walking shoes on this hike. The Northern Gateway of the STS is being moved back to the forestry office.

Start your hike at the gate on the road just beyond the garage. The road is blue-blazed as a cross-country ski trail. It bends first right, then left, where you turn right onto a blue-blazed trail that is part of the Ridge Trail. At 670 meters you reach the Susquehannock Trail. Please sign in at the trail register on your left but turn right onto the orange-blazed White Line Trail to continue your hike.

The White Line is a real trail and not a woods road like the Ridge Trail. To your left you see a clear-cut dating from 1985. The route of the STS is protected by a no-cut buffer. The cloverlike plant on the ground is oxalis or wood sorrel, and the toxic oxalic acid in its juice accounts for its sharp taste. Pioneers short of salt are said to have substituted an extract of oxalis; they must have been either desperate or unaware that oxalic acid is poisonous.

At 2.0 km you cross Lyman Run Road, then a jeep road, and next begin the long descent into Splash Dam Hollow. At the junction with Splash Dam Trail, the

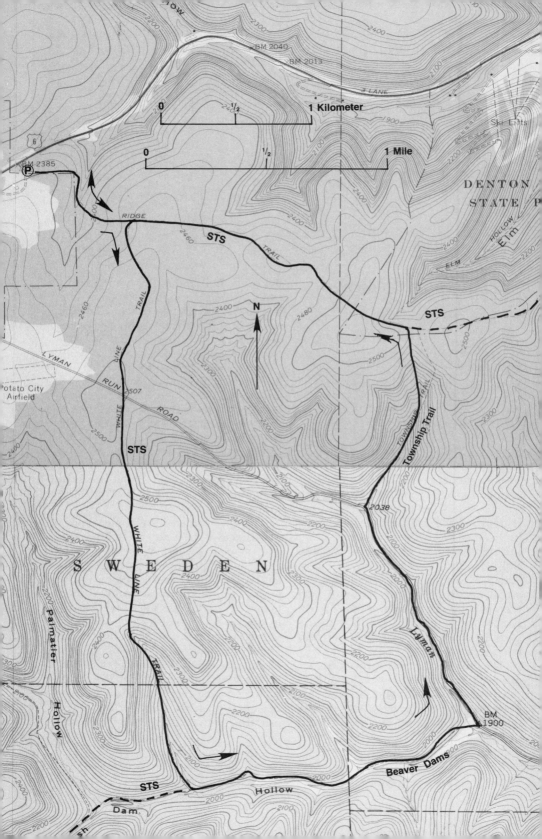

Ferns along the trail

Susquehannock turns right but you turn left. This trail, an easily followed old road, becomes even more distinct as you move downstream. Several beaver dams are visible along the stream, and these animals are probably responsible for the open meadows along the hollow. There is no sign of a splash dam but trout fishermen report old timbers in a deep pool near the junction with Lyman Run.

Splash dams were built on small streams to help float logs to sawmills. Most of them have rotted or been washed away. A well-preserved specimen can be seen on Eddy Lick Run (Hike 22).

At 6.2 km another old grade used by vehicles comes in from your left. Do not cross the stream, but continue ahead on the trail. A beaver dam has deepened the ford of Lyman Run, so detour upstream on a fisherman's path and cross above the pond. At 7.1 km turn left on Lyman Road.

At 8.9 km turn right on the unmarked and little-used Township Trail. At the time of my last visit there was no sign at this critical turn, just a post. When the footway becomes obscure, continue up the bottom of the hollow. Cross a new logging road at 10.1 km and continue almost due north through a broad, low place in the ridgetop. Turn left on the Susquehannock Trail at 10.4 km and proceed along the Ridge Trail to the junction with the blue-blazed trail at the trail register. Retrace your steps to the forestry office and your car at the Northern Gateway.

Allow time for a visit to the Pennsylvania Lumber Museum just across US 6 from Denton Hill State Park. Its exhibits will enhance your knowledge of the logging industry in this and other areas of Penn's Woods. Seeing the old Shay logging locomotive is itself worth the small admission price.

The Susquehannock Trail Map and Guide set is available from the Susquehannock Trail Club, PO Box 643, Coudersport, PA 16915. Write for the current price.

38

Baldwin Point

Distance: 11.8 km (7.3 miles)

Time: 4½ hours

Vertical Rise: 250 meters (820 ft)

Highlights: Views, Black Forest Trail

Maps: USGS 7.5' Slate Run; Black Forest Trail map

Highlights of this hike are views of the Baldwin Branch of Young Woman's Creek and Naval Run, a tributary of Pine Creek, plus a trek on a portion of the Black Forest Trail. Laid out with consummate skill by members of the Bureau of Forestry, the Black Forest Trail is aesthetically pleasing and extraordinarily scenic.

The name Black Forest was given to this region west of Pine Creek because its original evergreen forest resembled the Schwarzwald in southern Germany. The virgin stands of hemlock and red and white pine were so dense that sunlight did not reach the forest floor even at midday. The pines were the first to go. They were logged and floated down Pine Creek to the mills in Williamsport. When logging railroads were built here in the 1890s only the hemlocks and scattered hardwoods were left.

The Black Forest Trail was completed in 1971 and soon experienced the wear and tear of heavy use. The Baldwin Point Trail was blazed as a cross-country ski trail, but hikers are welcome to keep down the brush the rest of the year.

To reach the trailhead drive 11.3 miles north on PA 44 from the junction with PA 664 in Haneyville. After passing Benson Road on your left and Boyer Mills Road on your right, park in a small lot on the left side of PA 44 next to the gate blocking the trail to vehicles. There are some wet places and stream crossings where you will appreciate your hiking boots.

Head west on the blue-dot-blazed Baldwin Point Trail. You dip down into the headwaters of Yellow Jacket Hollow, passing close by two springs. You regain the plateau after a short climb and continue to a trail junction at 1.2 km where an unblazed trail leads left to the junction of Dry Run and Benson Roads. Turn right on the blue-blazed Baldwin Point Trail. Continue past the unblazed Old Refuge Trail at 2.3 km. On my last visit the sign at this junction had been stolen but there was another sign on the back of the tree.

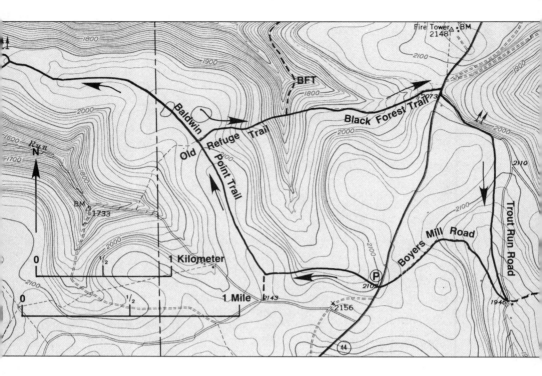

Next, the Baldwin Point Trail leads you through a stand of white birch to a vista at 4.5 km. Here you look west and north over the Baldwin and County Line branches of Young Woman's Creek, which flow into the West Branch of the Susquehanna at North Bend.

A grisly legend describes the naming of Young Woman's Creek. It is told that after a raid on the settlements, a Native American brave fled up the West Branch of the Susquehanna with a young woman captive. Fearing pursuit, he murdered her at the mouth of what is now called Young Woman's Creek and whenever he returned to this location he was haunted by her ghost.

Several specimens of red pine grow to one side of the overlook. These appear to be wild (that is, not planted) and at this point are fairly close to the southern limit of their range. Red pine seen much to the south of here usually have been planted.

To continue the hike, return to the junction with the unblazed Old Refuge Trail and turn left, or east, to follow it downhill into Yellow Jacket Hollow, where it joins the Black Forest Trail. The Black Forest Trail is blazed with orange dots, and you follow them up the other side of the hollow past a trail register.

Look for coyote scat along the BFT. It looks like fox scat but is larger and consists largely of hair. Despite having been hunted, poisoned, and trapped for over a century, coyotes have extended their range, filling in part the vacancy left by wolves. Indeed, eastern coyotes are about 15 percent wolf and weigh as much as 30 kg.

At 8.5 km you cross PA 44 and continue on Trout Run Road for 500 meters to a vista of Naval Run, Hemlock Mountain, and Gas Line Ridge. These areas are also visited or viewed on the Black Forest Trail (Hike 43). You now take the trail into the woods and soon cross and follow the headwaters of Trout Run. When you reach Boyers Mill Road turn right on this low-use, unpaved road. The sign here is in error by a factor of almost 2. It is only 1.3 km to PA 44, not 1.5 miles.

As soon as you approach PA 44, cut across the intervening ground and return to your car.

A map and guide set to the Black Forest Trail may be mail-ordered from the Tiadaghton Forest Fire Fighters Association, c/o Department of Environmental Resources, Bureau of Forestry, 423 East Central Avenue, South Williamsport, PA 17701. Write for the current price. For a camping permit call 717-327-3450.

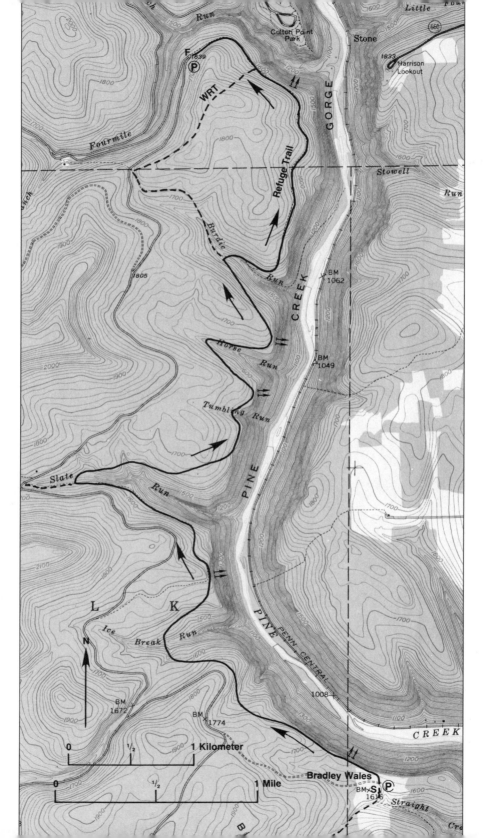

39

West Rim Trail

Distance: 12.0 km (7.5 miles)

Time: 4¼ hours

Vertical Rise: 185 meters (600 ft)

Highlights: Views

Maps: USGS 7.5' Tiadaghton; West Rim Trail

The northernmost part of Pine Creek Gorge, long a favorite with whitewater canoeists, offers hikers a breathtaking trail along the very edge of Pennsylvania's Grand Canyon. The Grand Canyon was created during the ice age when the continental ice sheet blocked drainage to the north. All the meltwater from a somewhat triangular portion of North America stretching far into Canada went through this gorge. As you see the tiny stream of today, try to imagine it then, its waters white with rock flour.

The hike described here requires a car shuttle. To reach the trailhead, turn south off US 6 at Ansonia and follow Colton Road past Colton Point State Park. At 6.5 miles from US 6 turn left

onto Painter Road, and at 8.3 miles turn left again onto Leetonia Road. Leave one car at the end of a switchback 9.1 miles from US 6. Then continue south on Leetonia Road 14.4 miles, turn left onto West Rim Road, and drive to the Bradley Wales Picnic Area, where you park. Hiking boots are your best bet on this hike.

Pick up the orange-blazed West Rim Trail at the woods on your right. At the edge of the canyon turn sharply left and move past a succession of views up, down, and across the gorge. Down the canyon, at the mouth of a hollow on the far side, you see a couple of cottages, the remains of the ghost town of Tiadaghton. In logging days it was a sizable town, with a sawmill and logging railroads spread far and wide.

At 900 meters, bear left away from the edge to head a nameless side stream and valley. This maneuver begins a trail pattern similar to that of the Tonto Trail in Arizona's Grand Canyon. If the side stream is small, a modest excursion is required to move around it; with a large stream the detour may be protracted.

After heading around this first side canyon, return briefly to the canyon's edge before swinging up Ice Break Run, which you cross at 2.2 km. Follow the trail back to the edge and a view. A blue-

Measuring distance on the West Rim Trail

blazed side trail here leads out to Leetonia Road. At 3 km bear left up Little Slate Run. This side canyon is the largest you encounter and offers a view across Little Slate.

At 4.5 km bear right off the old road. Another blue-blazed side trail leads out to Leetonia Road at this point. Cross Little Slate Run and turn downstream on the far side. You quickly pick up another old grade and climb to a side stream of Little Slate Run. At 6.1 km you are back at the edge. Cross Tumbling Run, and reach another view.

Horse Run requires only a modest detour but the crossing requires a sharp descent and then a steep scramble back up. By 8 km you are back at the edge (and another view) with a clear footway ahead. At 8.8 km jog left on a woods road and cross Burdic Run. The blue-blazed road continues left and leads out to Leetonia Road.

Watch the blazes carefully on the far side of Burdic Run as the trail climbs the bank and bears right to an old grade which returns to the run farther downstream. At 9.1 km pick up the Refuge Trail. This trail, like others of the same name around the state, marked a game refuge boundary. Such refuges were once common but most have now been abandoned. They were usually established in blissful ignorance of the size and diversity of land required for the home range of the animals they were to protect.

After a short climb the Refuge Trail levels to an old railroad grade. Pass a view of Colton Point State Park and continue on the blue-blazed railroad grade where the orange-blazed West Run Trail (WRT) turns left uphill. Follow the blue-blazed trail up Four Mile Run to the switchback on Leetonia Road and your car.

Write to Tioga State Forest, Box 94, Route 287S, Wellsboro, PA 16901 for a copy of the West Rim Trail map. For a camping permit call 717-724-2868.

40

Bucktail Path

Distance: 12.7 km (7.9 miles)

Time: 4¾ hours

Vertical Rise: 128 meters (420 ft)

Highlights: Mountain stream, beaver ponds

Maps: USGS 7.5' Emporium, Wharton; Elk State Forest Public Use Map

Here is a hike that will challenge your pathfinding ability. It certainly should not be your first adventure in Penn's Woods, nor should you attempt it if you don't like to stray off the beaten path. The Bucktail Path, which extends from the village of Sinnemahoning on PA 120 to Sizerville State Park on PA 155, was for many years one of the least used trails in Penn's Woods. In recent years it has been reblazed and cleared by the Trail Care Team of the Keystone Trails Association. As a result usage has picked up on the Bucktail. It is is not to be confused with the nearby Bucktail Trail, which consists of PA 120 from Lockhaven to Emporium. This hike uses the section of the

Bucktail Path along the McNuff Branch of Hunts Run. The trailhead is 4.8 miles up Hunts Run Road from PA 120 at the village of Cameron. Cameron is 12 miles north of Driftwood and 6 miles south of Emporium. In Cameron turn right, cross the stream, and then turn left. Park at the side of the road near the Bucktail Path sign. There are stream crossings and a number of wet spots along the route of this in-and-out hike, so your hiking boots are in order. Also make sure your compass is in your pack.

To start, head into the woods and follow the blazes upstream. The bridge over Hunts Run is gone, so cross as best you can. Turn sharply left onto trail. A hunting camp is visible to your right as you cross a meadow. Soon it becomes apparent that you are following an old road grade, and the McNuff Branch comes into view. On many parts of the Bucktail Path there is at least an intermittent footway. You next come to a section where the old grade has been washed out and you must scramble up the hillside to get around. Farther along you'll see a number of spruce trees which may well have been planted by the Civilian Conservation Corps 60 years ago.

At 2.7 km there is a bridgeless crossing of the McNuff Branch. This crossing is

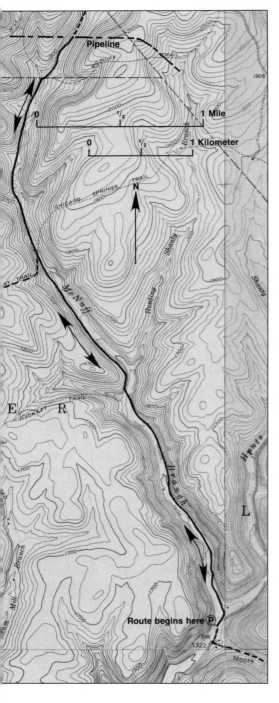

well marked. On the far side you will find another old grade. Turn right and follow it to a wet area. Then look up the slope to your left for the next blaze. The trail continues a little way up the slope. Below you is a dense stand of hemlocks.

As you proceed up the valley the footway is fairly well defined and easier to follow than it was before the crossing. The hemlocks give way to hardwoods and these are interspersed with open meadows. At 4.5 km you cross the unsigned and poorly defined Mowray Trail.

After crossing a side stream at 5.0 km, keep left along the base of the slope to pick up the trail again. After a dry hollow, look for an active beaver dam. At 6.0 km you cross another side stream; note a spring that emerges below the trail.

You reach the Consolidated Gas and Supply pipeline at 6.4 km. The Bucktail Path continues to the Steam Mill Road and then to Sizerville State Park, but your hike turns back at this point. Retrace your steps to your car, avoiding the Mowray Trail.

A map of the Bucktail Path may be available one of these days, but until then it is shown best on the public use map of Elk State Forest. This can be obtained by writing to Elk State Forest, RD #1, Route 155, Box 327, Emporium, PA 15834. For a camping permit call 814-486-3353.

41

Golden Eagle Trail

Distance: 14.4 km (8.9 miles)

Time: 6 hours

Vertical Rise: 640 meters (2100 ft)

Highlights: Views, waterfalls

Maps: USGS 7.5' Cammal, Slate Run;
Golden Eagle Trail map

The Golden Eagle Trail may be the best day hike in Penn's Woods. It has everything: mountain streams, big trees, mountain laurel, relics from the logging days, views of wild and pastoral landscapes, meadows, small waterfalls, and, of course, Pine Creek. Overnight camping is not permitted on this rugged trail since the few available sites would suffer from overuse. If there is snow or ice on the ground do not attempt this trail without crampons.

The trail is on State Game Land 68 and in Tiadaghton State Forest, where it traverses the Wolf Run Wild Area. To reach the trail, drive north on PA 414 for 2.7 miles beyond the village of Cammal and park on the roadside. A large post

sign marks the trailhead. Wear your hiking boots for this excursion in Penn's Woods.

You begin the trail, marked with low-profile, circular orange blazes, by crossing the former railroad grade and climbing a ledge. Turn left and cross Wolf Run on a culvert. Then turn right past a trail register and proceed up Wolf Run. You next pass an old quarry and the junction with the return portion of the trail. Continue up the run. Crossings are now fairly frequent, and you see several small waterfalls along here.

At 1.3 km in the hollow on your left you see remains of an old log skid. Logs were often slid down the sides of steep hills to a railroad or a stream for transportation to Williamsport. At 2.3 km Watson Fork comes in from the east with Wolf Rock, a natural overlook, to its south. No trail runs to Wolf Rock but if you move up Watson Fork a short distance and then scramble up the steep slope to your right, you can reach the top. If the trees have dropped their leaves, you will have a good view of Wolf Run Valley.

At 3.4 km you reach an old logging camp marked by large white pines and hemlocks and the remains of the old camp stove. Evidently the loggers were

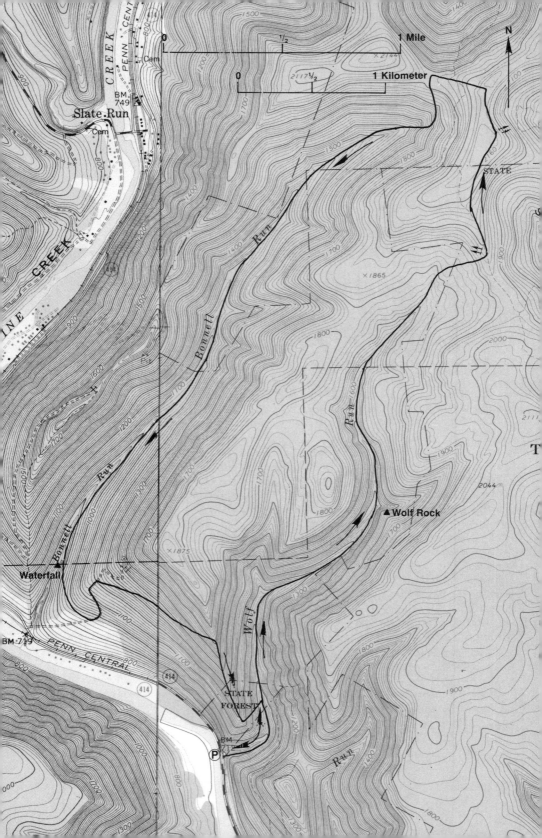

Field and mountains on the Golden Eagle Trail

reluctant to cut trees in the immediate vicinity of their camp. Wolf Run becomes intermittent above this point. You soon move out of the hollow and reach—at 4.7 km—the first vista to look west over the top of Wolf Run and across Bonnell Run to Black Forest Trail country on the far side of Pine Creek.

You then continue up the ridgeline and cross into State Game Land 68 for a view east over the fields of Beulahland. At 665 meters this is the highest point on the trail. At 6 km, turn left for a second view west across Bonnell Run to Black Forest Trail country. The Golden Eagle Trail then slants down into the saddle, where it turns left into Bonnell Run. Continue down Bonnell Run and cross back into state forest at 9.5 km. Soon the run enters a small gorge and you veer slowly away from it on an old grade. At 11.1 km you bear left on the trail. At this point a small waterfall lies at the bottom

of a steep descent to Bonnell Run. Back on the trail you now climb gently to the edge of Clark's Pasture for a view down Pine Creek, then follow the field's edge to an old quarry road, and begin a serious climb to the ridge between Wolf Run and Pine Creek at 12.7 km.

The first vista to the left of the trail has a good view up Wolf Run. The second vista is from a rock called the Raven's Horn, which is a roosting spot for ravens and has views of both Wolf Run and Pine Creek. The third and last vista has views up and down Pine Creek. You then descend on steep switchbacks before turning left off the ridge into Wolf Run. Continue descending to the trail, coming up Wolf Run at 13.9 km. Turn right for the brief journey back to PA 414.

The Golden Eagle Trail map is available free from the Bureau of Forestry, 423 East Central Avenue, South Williamsport, PA 17701.

42

Pine Trail and Hemlock Mountain

Distance: 15.4 km (9.6 miles)

Time: 6 hours

Vertical Rise: 580 meters (1900 ft)

Highlights: Views, mountain streams, waterfall

Maps: USGS 7.5' Slate Run; Black Forest Trail

This hike is the real Pine Creek experience. Pine Trail and Hemlock Mountain have it all—views, a waterfall, lots of change in elevation, cliffs, and, of course, Pine Creek. Because of the climb up Riffle Run and the length of this hike, you should not attempt it as a first hike if you have a fear of heights or if there is ice or snow on the ground. This hike uses parts of the Black Forest Trail as well as side trails, both blazed and unblazed, and a long section of a low-use forest road.

The trailhead is at the end of Naval Run Road across Pine Creek from the vil-

lage of Slate Run on PA 414. From downtown Slate Run, cross the bridge over Pine Creek and turn left on Naval Run Road at the far side. It is 1.2 miles to the end of the road, where there is parking space for quite a few cars. You will want your hiking boots on this hike, for footing on the narrow footway above Pine Creek and for the rocks farther up Riffle Run.

Your hike starts on the Pine Trail at a sign at the end of the road. Pine Trail is blazed with blue rectangles. You descend immediately to Naval Run and cross as best you can on rocks. Then you climb to an open area where you turn left on an old road that parallels Pine Creek in a pleasant green tunnel through stands of hemlocks.

At 1.2 km you cross Callahan Run on rocks and turn upstream on the far side, picking up an old road grade among white pines. The grade follows Callahan Run, but just before the valley closes in you turn left. Move carefully from one blaze to the next as there is little footway here. Soon the hillside becomes steeper; the trail has been cut into the side of the hill. After crossing a dry run you reach a series of cliffs. The trail skirts the bottom of these outcrops with a fair amount of up and down. The slope has become steeper and if you dislodge a stone it will

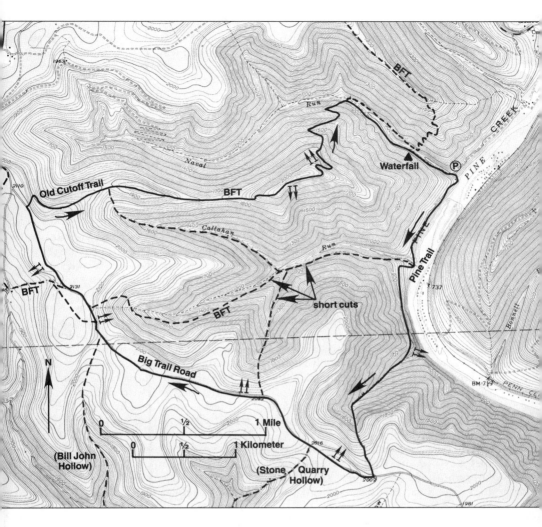

probably go all the way to Pine Creek below. Be glad you are only carrying a day pack. Finally you must bend over and crawl through a notch in the last cliff to emerge at the corner of Riffle Run Valley at 2.3 km. There is a good view here, both down and across Pine Creek. The view is even better from a ledge a few meters above the trail.

Pine Trail then swings up Riffle Run Valley and soon picks up an old grade, starting a relentless climb. The grade becomes fainter and there are repeated stream crossings. Farther up, the valley splits and you bear left. The route here has many loose rocks and little trace of footway. Soon you pass the last water and see an edge above you. The climbing eases off above this edge but continues through mountain laurel all the way to Big Trail Road at 4.0 km.

Turn right on this dead-end, little-used road, which follows the top of a ridge between Trout Run to the west and Pine Creek and its tributaries to the east. It is regrettable that Big Trail was ever downgraded into a road.

Sc n you reach a view over Riffle Run and up Pine Creek Valley past the village of Slate Run. After you have climbed Riffle Run the steep-sided valley is a matter of direct experience.

As you continue along Big Trail Road, watch the surface for fragments of vegetable material covered with spines. No, these are not porcupine eggshells; they are burrs from occasional American chestnuts that still grow in Penn's Woods. When you find such burrs, look carefully at the trees along the roadside to identify the chestnut. In season it will have long, bladelike leaves edged with pointed teeth. Chances are that if you examine the trunk you will find it already bears a chestnut blight canker.

Next you pass a woods road to your left that goes down Stone Quarry Hollow to Trout Run. At 5.5 km you reach a trail on your right that descends the left fork of Callahan Run, which you could use to truncate this hike by turning down Callahan Run to Pine Trail.

You pass another view up Pine Creek just beyond the Callahan Trail and later another trail on the left that leads to Trout Run, this time via Bill John Hollow.

At 7.4 km the orange-blazed Black Forest Trail (BFT) emerges from the woods on your left across from an extensive view of Hemlock Mountain to the east. The Black Forest Trail continues along the road for 100 meters before it turns right and descends the middle fork of Callahan Run, offering a last opportunity to truncate the hike.

Next you pass a nameless trail to the left; at 8.1 km there is a view left over the headwaters of Trout Run. Then watch carefully on your right for the unblazed Old Cutoff Trail. This junction is signed and marked with a log gate, but should you miss it you will soon reach Trout Run Road.

Turn right on the Old Cutoff Trail, which is easy to follow even without markings. It first bears west before heading east down the crest of Hemlock Mountain.

You join the Black Forest Trail in a saddle at 9.7 km. Continue ahead on the Black Forest Trail along the ridgetop. As you ascend the peak, stop and look back at views over Callahan Run.

At 11.8 km you reach a view south along Pine Creek. This is one of the three or four best views on the Black Forest Trail. On a clear day the last ridge that you can see on the horizon is North White Deer, about 45 km away. Notice how straight Pine Creek Valley is. Presumably, Pine Creek Valley follows an ancient fault through the Allegheny Plateau.

Now the trail starts to descend and soon reaches a view to the north. The trail next swings off the ridgeline and switchbacks down the steep north face of Hemlock Mountain. Near the top it passes through a stand of the hemlocks that give the mountain its name. Several old log skids are connected by new trail on the way down to Naval Run. Near the bottom the unblazed Horse Path goes straight ahead and provides a shortcut to Naval Run Road.

At 13.9 km, turn right onto the old Naval Run Road. Hike 43 is on the far side of Naval Run. Next, you pass above Naval Run Falls. When I passed this way during Hurricane Agnes in 1972, the ground shook beneath my feet from the power of the falls.

About 300 meters beyond the falls, look for the ruins of a culvert in Naval Run. Cross Naval Run as best you can at this point and ascend the old road on the far side to the parking area at the end of Naval Run Road.

Nearby hiking opportunities include the Black Forest Trail (Hike 43), the Golden Eagle Trail (Hike 41), and Baldwin Point (Hike 38).

A map and guide set to the Black Forest Trail may be mail-ordered from the Tiadaghton Forest Fire Fighters Association, c/o Department of Environmental Resources, Bureau of Forestry, 423 East Central Avenue, South Williamsport, PA 17701. Write for the current price.

43

Black Forest Trail

Distance: 15.8 km (9.8 miles)

Time: 5½ hours

Vertical Rise: 370 meters (1220 ft)

Highlights: Views, waterfall

Maps: USGS 7.5' Slate Run; Black Forest Trail map

This hike treats you to a section of the famous Black Forest Trail along Pine Creek Gorge. Your route goes past a waterfall, views, and the historic remains of the Cammal and Black Forest Railroad, built to log much of this area.

The hike's trailhead was once a pumping station on the Tidewater Petroleum pipeline, the first successful long-distance pipeline in the world, built by independent oil producers in an attempt to circumvent John D. Rockfeller's monopoly of the railroads. The pumps here were powered by a steam engine; coal to fire it was transported on the Cammal and Black Forest Railroad. When the railroad ceased operating, a natural gas well was drilled at Slate Run and a short pipe-line was run from there to the pump station to keep the steam engine going. The Tidewater pipeline, tiny by today's standards, is now used for optical fiber communications, but you can see remains of it in several road cuts along PA 44, particularly to the north of the pump station. The pipeline was built in 1879 but the pump station was presumably built later, as the Cammal and Black Forest didn't reach it until 1894 or 1895.

To reach the trailhead drive north on PA 44 for 12.9 miles from the junction with PA 664 in Haneyville. Turn right on the Manor Fork Road, drive past a couple of hunting camps, and park at the winter sports parking area at the far side of the clearing. Hiking boots are in order for this excursion.

Start walking on Manor Fork Road and then bear right on a trail with blue blazes at the vehicle gate. This is the Gas Line Trail, which follows the route of the old gas pipeline from Slate Run. Along this section you pass an obscure junction with your return route.

At 2.0 km you continue ahead on the orange-blazed Black Forest Trail, which comes in from the left. After 200 meters turn left to reach White Birch Lookout. This vista is a bit off the main trail but don't pass it by unless the ridge is really

Fast water in early spring

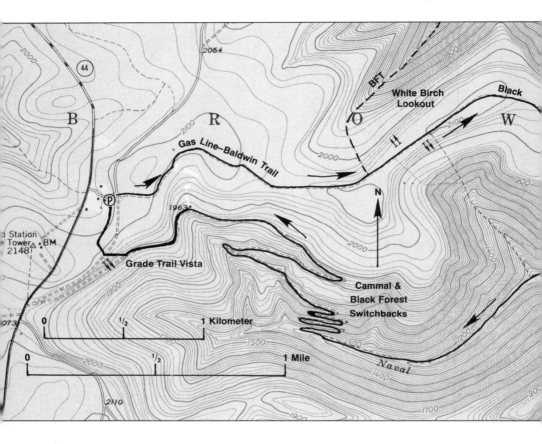

socked in with dense fog. White Birch looks north over Little Slate Run Valley. Moss Hollow Lookout, another 200 meters or so along the trail, looks south over Naval Run to Hemlock Mountain. At 3.3 km you bear right to reach Canyon Vista. In front of you the ground falls away into Naval Run, revealing Pine Creek, the famous gorge, far to the south, and the hills beyond. This is one of the three or four best views on the Black Forest Trail.

When you can tear yourself away from Canyon Vista, continue past Naval Run View to the west and Lookout Ledge, where you see Pine Creek Gorge to the north, along with the tiny village of Slate Run. Next is a view of Hemlock Mountain to the southwest. You then bear right and switchback down into Naval Run.

At the bottom, head upstream above Naval Run. The waterfall, at 7.2 km, is visible from the trail, but you have to descend the steep bank to the edge of the overhang to get a really good look. This part of the state was never glaciated and waterfalls are rare.

At 8.2 km you leave the trail where it crosses the run. Don't cross; instead continue upstream as best you can for some 50 meters, then bear right on the wide but unblazed fire road that crosses the run at this point. Heading upstream, you follow the delightful little stream as it

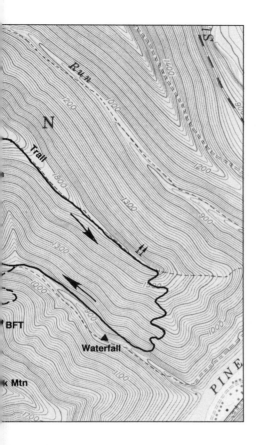

the spur at the second switchback, only two log cars at a time could have been brought up this grade. The third switchback has been complicated by quarrying operations. A quarry road continues ahead but is steeper and less smooth than the old railroad grade. Turn sharply right again and follow the grade through one quarry and then above another one. From here on it is smooth sailing past the fourth, fifth, and sixth switchbacks.

At 14.8 km you reach a berm across the old grade. Continue ahead to a blue-blazed trail on your right just before a clearing. A sign at this junction directs you to the Pump Station Parking Area. Climb this trail to another switchback of the C & BF Railroad above and turn left to Grade Trail Vista. The view looks east over Naval Run and Hemlock Mountain. Then follow the blue blazes through the woods, and in 600 meters you are back at your car.

A map and guide set to the Black Forest Trail may be mail-ordered from the Tiadaghton Forest Fire Fighters Association, c/o Department of Environmental Resources, Bureau of Forestry, 423 East Central Avenue, South Williamsport, PA 17701. Write for the current price. For a camping permit call 717-327-3450.

tinkles over the moss-covered rocks and sparkles in the sun.

Your next turn onto railroad switchbacks is not marked and requires special attention. As you walk up the fire road along the run you cross a side stream from Moss Hollow. Continue ahead for over a kilometer and then start looking uphill on your right to find the old railroad grade coming down. It reaches the bottom at a dry run on your right. (The fire road continues upstream past this point.)

Take a sharp right onto the railroad grade at this first switchback and start your easy but protracted climb out of Naval Run. Judging from the length of

44

Asaph Wild Area

Distance: 15.9 km (9.9 miles)

Time: 6 hours

Vertical Rise: 390 meters (1270 ft)

Highlights: Hessel Gesser Millstone

Map: USGS 7.5' Asaph

In the northern reaches of Tioga State Forest lie a small wild area and contiguous natural area that provide the setting for a challenging day hike—but not if it's your first time out. You need skill in following unblazed trails and making one short bushwhack. Some of the trail junctions on this hike are marked only with signs, so you may feel better with your compass in your pack.

The circuit hike begins and ends at the Asaph Run State Forest Picnic Area at the forks of Asaph Run. The area is reached from US 6 between PA 287 and PA 362. Turn north over Marsh Creek at the sign for Asaph Village from the west or Fish Hatchery from the east. Cross Marsh Creek immediately and proceed 0.2 mile farther to a stop sign. Turn left,

and after another 0.5 mile turn right just before the road recrosses the railroad tracks. Drive 2.7 miles to the picnic area. There is a parking area to your right and more parking space and a camping area on the far side of Asaph Run. Wear your hiking boots on this outing.

To start your hike cross Right Asaph Run as best you can and head up the unblazed Middle Ridge Trail. Left Asaph Run drops below, and occasionally you glimpse the canyon's far side. At 1.5 km take the trail's left fork and farther along keep right at the edge of a clearing with old apple trees. The trees suggest this was once a logging camp. The grade up the side of the middle ridge is too variable for a logging railroad. Ignore the well-used Big Tree Hollow Trail on your left. By 4.9 km you see you are on an old railroad grade.

On the top of Middle Ridge, you will pick up blue blazes. Then ignore the Johnson Trail, also on your left. Heavy use by horses has produced extensive mud holes that in wet weather become long mud puddles. Next, the old grade bends right onto a recent logging road. Follow the blue blazes where they bear left off this road and reach the outlet from Black Ash Swamp. Fresh beaver workings here have deepened the stream.

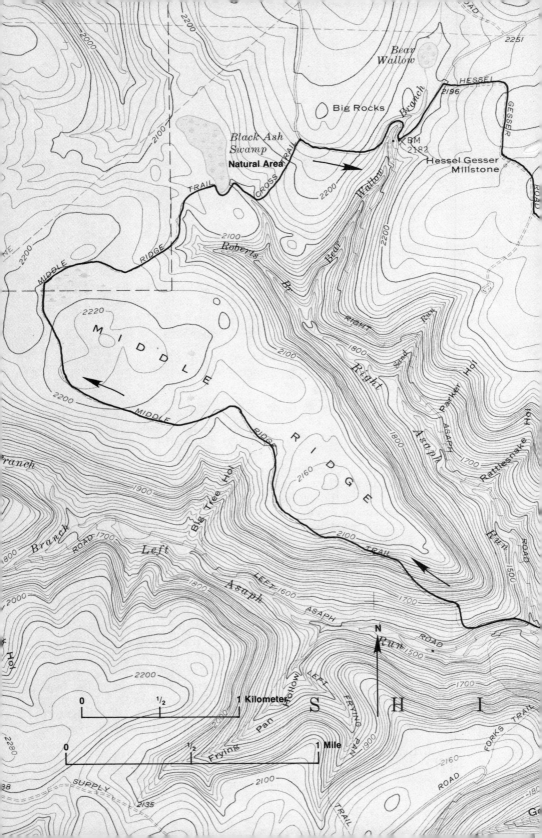

At the time of my visit the best bet was to cross downstream below the last dam. On the other side pass a trail sign and continue up the Cross Trail on the edge of an extensive clear-cut. The blazes stop at 7.4 km, where you turn right on Right Asaph Road for 900 meters to a junction with Sand Road. (To shorten your hike, turn right down Right Asaph Road.) To continue, turn left up Sand Road, and after 500 meters turn right on Hessel Gesser Road.

After 1.0 km watch on your right for an outcrop of coarse sandstone and conglomerate. This is the site of the Hessel Gesser Millstone, which is marked with a large signboard. In the 1830s James Hessel Gesser cut stones here for gristmills in Tioga and Potter Counties. This blank evidently had no buyer. Gristmills were not a runaway success, and according to county records, those in Tioga County soon closed "for lack of a profitable clientele."

Hessel Gesser Road is gated to vehicles just beyond the millstone, but you continue, and just before the road swings right in a clearing bear left on the signed Scotch Pine Hollow Trail. This trail shows use by horses, but as you swing along the broad ridgetop the trail narrows. Ignore another trail to your left. Then you encounter a small run flowing left across the trail toward Straight Run. Continue past Darling Road Trail on your left at 12.5 km to descend into Scotch Pine Hollow. Shortly, you cross the run, bear left at a fork at 13.8 km, and at 14.5 km you come to Asaph Road.

Turn right on the road and walk 1.4 km back to your car. Along the way you pass another, steeper version of the Scotch Pine Hollow Trail that follows the run down to the road.

45

Hammersley Wild Area

Distance: 17.5 km (10.9 miles)	
Time: 6 hours	
Vertical Rise: 275 meters (900 ft)	
Highlights: Large wild area	
Maps: USGS 7.5' Conrad, Short Run, Tamarack; Susquehannock Trail Map 5	

Your trek here is through one of the largest roadless areas in the state. The Susquehannock Trail traverses the Hammersley Wild Area and this is the longest section (16 km) that does not cross a road.

The Hammersley was not always so wild. At the turn of the century it was laced with railroads and even supported a town where the Nelson Branch joins the Hammersley Fork. Most of the trails through the wild area are old railroad grades.

The Hammersley is widely known for its rattlesnakes. About half of all the rattlesnakes I've encountered in Penn's Woods have been here, so do watch your step.

You need a car shuttle. Leave one car in the hikers' lot in the village of Cross Fork on PA 144, just north of the Clinton-Potter county line. (At the turn of the century, this tiny town had scheduled rail service, stave and lumber mills, and a population of thousands.) To reach the other end of this hike, from Cross Fork follow PA 144 left for over 0.5 mile, and then turn right on Cross Fork Creek Road for 3.9 miles. Turn left on Windfall Road and drive for 3.8 miles to Red Ridge Road, and turn left. After another 3.6 miles, turn left yet again onto McConnell Road. About 2 miles down the road you pass a vista of the upper Hammersley area and Elk Lick Knob. The Susquehannock Trail crossing is just 0.3 mile farther, before you reach the bottom of the saddle. You can park along the road. Hiking boots are in order for this extra-vehicular activity.

Start your hike down the orange-blazed Hammersley Trail, as the Susquehannock is here called. After 1.3 km, you reach the first of a series of meadows. Note the apple trees, which legends say grew from apple cores thrown away by lumberjacks.

A pipeline swath is crossed at 2.3 km. Wild area designation protects the Hammersley from crossings by any more such rights-of-way. Soon you pass Black

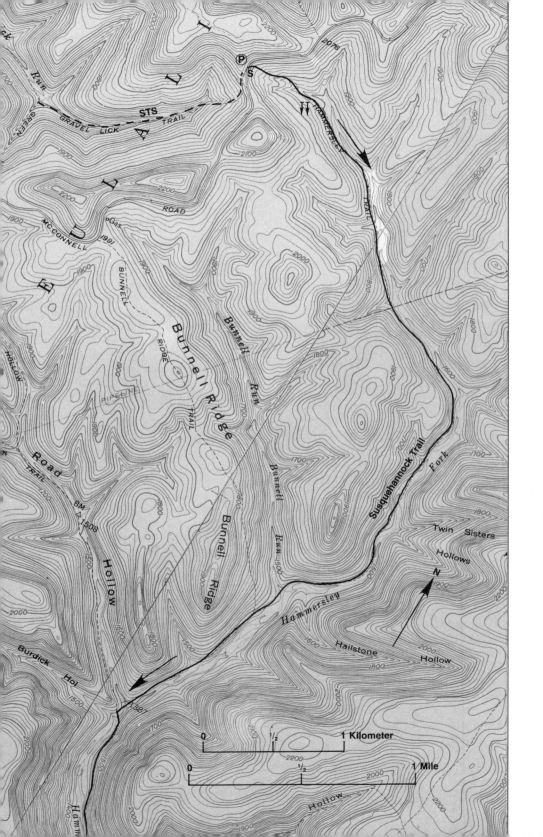

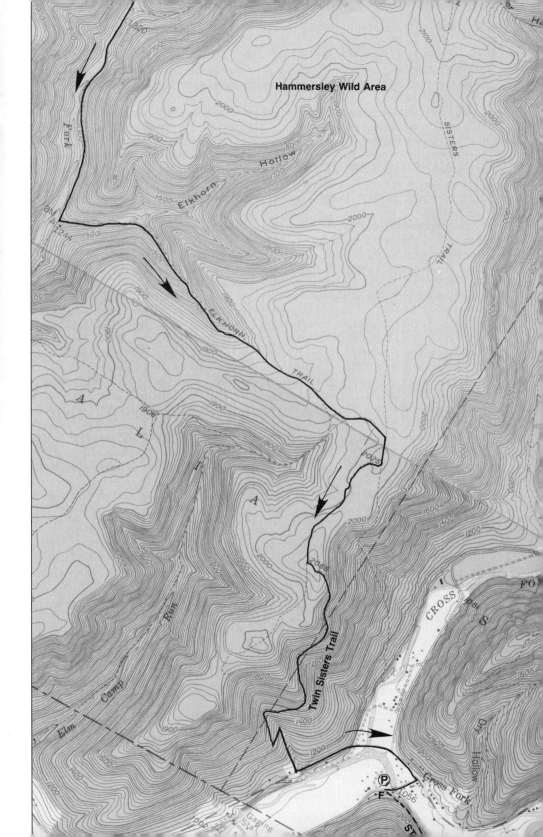

Hammersley Wild Area

Mark Hollow, named for a black mark made by Native Americans on a tree at the hollow's mouth.

Stonework bridge abutments are still visible at several places where the old railroad grade crosses side streams. You cross Bunnell Run at 5.3 km and shortly the Bunnell Ridge Trail, and then Road Hollow Run and its trail at 6.7 km. Road Hollow is named for the railroad that ran here.

Shortly you cross the Hammersley Fork itself. Most of the season you can hop on rocks but in higher water you might have to wade across. Scramble up the steep bank on the far side. The trail stays well up the side of the valley from here to Dry Hollow, at 8.1 km. Despite its name a good flow of water usually exits from Dry Hollow, and at one time there was a splash dam here.

Just beyond, you reach a cascade and pool, one of the gems of the Hammersley. The water here is deep enough for swimming even in midsummer. Downstream from this pool you climb again, pass a trail register, and finally return to water level at the mouth of Elkhorn Hollow.

Here you follow the blazes left uphill on the Elkhorn Trail and start the big climb of the day. At first you follow the run, but at 10.3 km you bear right up a steep bank and start the real climb. Toward the top the grade eases off, but you continue climbing until 12.2 km.

Shortly after reaching the crest you bear right onto the Twin Sisters Trail, named for Twin Sisters Hollow, which in turn was named for two giant pines that once grew there. Now you can really swing along through the luxuriant thickets of mountain laurel. The former vista at 14.2 km is grown over.

From here it's all downhill along the old Lackawanna Lumber Company railroad grade. Near the bottom the trail switchbacks left into a small hollow. The trail emerges on PA 144 at the junction with Cross Fork Creek Road. Turn left on PA 144. Continue along the highway and turn right on the road to Cross Fork to return to your car in the hikers' parking lot.

The Susquehannock Trail map can be mail-ordered from the club. Write Susquehannock Trail Club, PO Box 643, Coudersport, PA 16915 for the current price. Call Susquehannock State Forest at 814-274-8474 for a camping permit.

BACKPACKING TRIPS

46

Worlds End State Park

Distance: 28.0 km (17.4 miles)

Time: 2 days, 1 night

Vertical Rise: 830 meters (2720 ft)

Highlights: Views, waterfalls

*Maps: USGS 7.5' Eagles Mere;
Loyalsock Trail Map 3*

Worlds End State Park is located in the Loyalsock Canyon of Sullivan County. The rugged, demanding Loyalsock Trail, laid out in the early 1950s by Explorer Scouts from Williamsport, traverses the park. Despite many relocations their predilection for steep climbs is still apparent. A marked side trail, RX-8, known as the Link Trail, makes possible a 2-day circuit backpack from Worlds End State Park. The Alpine Club of Williamsport (PO Box 501, Williamsport, PA 17703) and the concession stand in the park sell a map and guide set to the Loyalsock Trail.

The best way to get to Worlds End State Park is from US 220 at Laporte, by driving west on PA 154 for 7.3 miles. The park can also be reached from PA 87 at Forksville, again via PA 154. Leave your car at the park office; you will enjoy the hike more knowing that the park security force is keeping an eye on your car. Check in at the office for parking instructions. You will certainly want your hiking boots for this rugged trail. For a camping permit call Wyoming State Forest at 717-387-4255.

First Day
*Worlds End State Park to Sones
Pond
Distance: 12.6 km (7.8 miles)
Time: 5½ hours*

The Loyalsock Trail passes in front of the park office, but it is more rewarding to follow the yellow blazes marking the High Rock Run Trail. Your route follows the edge of Loyalsock Creek. Leave the trail here for a good view of the cliff carved into High Rock by the creek and also the waterfall on High Rock Run. Your hike will soon take you above both these features.

High Rock Run Trail soon rejoins the Loyalsock Trail, which is marked with yellow and red paint blazes of superior quality. You pass a sign identifying the lowest point in Sullivan County, implying that you have nowhere to go from here but up! Next, bear left on a road bridge across Loyalsock Creek, passing the junction with the Link Trail where you will return tomorrow. At the far end of the bridge turn left onto trail and start to climb. Cross a footbridge over High Rock Run at 1.1 km and then turn sharply right. Avoid the old trail that goes straight ahead at this turn. It passes dangerously close to the brink of the cliff and at least two hikers have fallen to their deaths from it. Here the route becomes so steep that I wished I was carrying an internal frame pack in order to keep my balance. You reach High Rock Vista at 1.6 km with a commanding view across the park to Canyon Vista, where you will be tomorrow.

Here you leave the yellow markers of High Rock Run Trail and turn right on the Loyalsock Trail. Continue to climb an old road grade. After crossing the white-blazed park boundary you traverse a tract of land recently acquired by the North Central Pennsylvania Conservancy and transferred to Wyoming State Forest. At 2.2 km you pass a spring that emerges from under a tree, and at 3.0 km you jog right on Loyalsock Road, crossing High Rock Run before turning left on High Rock Spur, which is obviously an old logging railroad grade. Hemlock, beech, chestnut oak, and white pine line the path. At 4.2 km turn right onto an old logging road and at 5.3 km cross Loyalsock Road again. Beyond, you pass the remains of a beaver pond, cross Big Run, and then bear right on a railroad grade. You come to a view down Big Run called Ken's Window at 7.0 km. Next, you circle around the top of a landslide that may have carried away the old railroad grade. Above Tom's Run you pick up what may be the same grade and follow it upstream past a campsite toward Alpine Falls. At

7.5 km drop your pack and continue upstream on a red-X trail for a view of Alpine Falls. Then retrace your steps and follow the main trail to its crossing of Tom's Run above the falls. Beyond, continue climbing and cross a couple of old logging roads.

At 9.6 km jog left on the Loyalsock Road and then cross Tamarack Run at 10.3 km. This spot is known as "Ann's Bridge" but it is actually only a step over the stream. Next climb through some large rocks known as Porky Den. The trail continues on a series of old woods roads, crossing a small stream at 11.4 km and the inlet to Sones Pond at 12.4 km. Get your water here rather than from Sones Pond itself. There are several campsites along the shore.

Second Day
Sones Pond to Worlds End State Park
Distance: 15.4 km (9.6 miles)
Time: 8 hours

The trail continues along the shore of Sones Pond before turning left through a spruce plantation along Rock Run Road, which you cross at 13.0 km. Beyond, continue to the edge of the Loyalsock Canyon, where you descend along rock ledges. Then pick up a woods road, which is on a level bench. At 14.8 km turn right and descend steeply along an old log skid. There is a small stream to your left.

Turn right on graveled Haystacks Road, follow it out to Rock Run Road, and turn left. Civilian Conservation Corps Camp 95 was on the flood plain upstream from the iron bridge across Loyalsock Creek. The campers were responsible for building Sones Pond, where you camped last night. On the far side of the bridge turn right on the red-X trail and cross a bridge over Mill Creek.

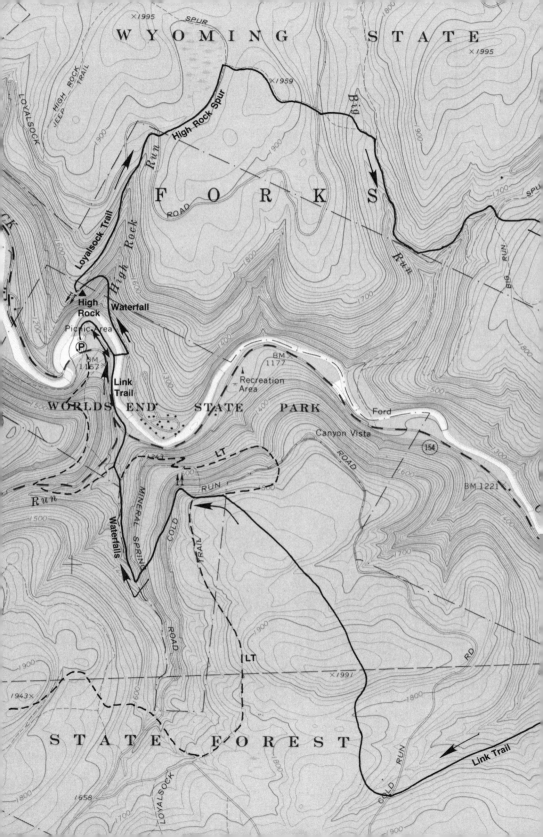

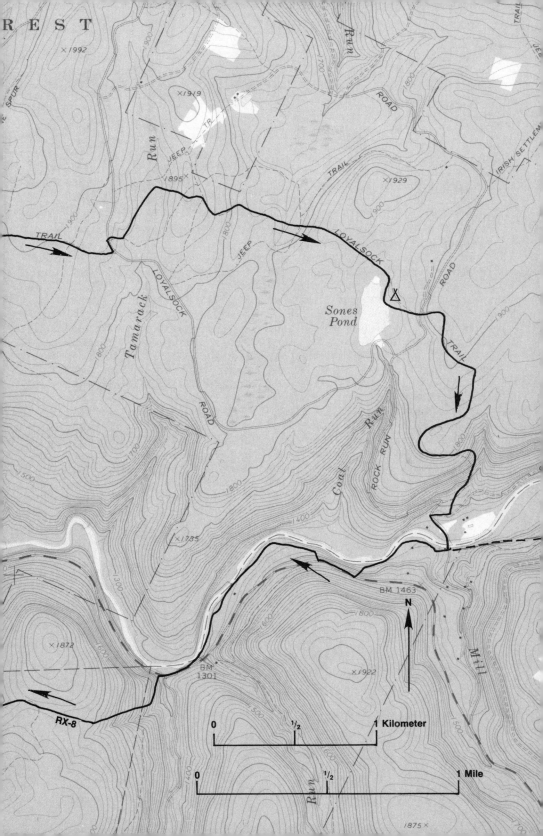

The Link Trail then takes you along the edge of Loyalsock Creek. At one point you traverse wet, slippery rocks at the base of a cliff. In high water you might have to detour up to the highway to get around this section.

The Link Trail continues downstream with occasional views of the creek. Cross Pole Bridge Run on rocks and continue along the edge of the creek to 18.4 km, where you bear right on PA 154. Cross Shanerburg Run on the highway bridge and then turn left on an old grade. You soon reach the end of the grade and turn right for some serious climbing. At 19.3 km you bear right on a woods road and continue climbing, but gently now. Compared with the main stem of the Loyalsock Trail, the Link Trail is little traveled. The Link Trail continues on a number of old grades, but at 20.1 km turn left on a logging road and follow it past several springs.

At 21.5 km you pass a gate, cross Cold Run Road, and continue on the Link Trail. Soon you cross Cold Run and an old road. At 22.6 km you reach the top of hill 1991 and continue through the woods, crossing streams at 23.1 km and 23.4 km and passing a spring at 24.0 km. Turn left on the Loyalsock Trail at 24.4 km and make your way carefully along the edge of these rocks. Follow the Loyalsock Trail across Cold Run Road to Canyon Vista.

A relic of the logging era along the Loyalsock

Beyond the vista, the Link Trail diverges from the Loyalsock Trail and descends into the valley of Double Run. Following the Link Trail, you cross Mineral Spring Road at 25.6 km and then follow Double Run downstream. The trail leads over and around boulders, and I found myself wishing for an internal frame pack again; however, the falls and cascades of Double Run are well worth your exertions.

At 26.1 km you pick up an old logging railroad grade, and soon you turn left on the Loyalsock Trail again. Cross both branches of Double Run and then continue ahead where the Loyalsock Trail turns left. Cross PA 154 at 26.9 km and then make your way along the edge of Loyalsock Creek to the bridge. Here you turn left and retrace your steps to the park office.

47

Hyner Run to Ole Bull

Distance: 36.3 km (22.6 miles)

Time: 2 days, 1 night

Vertical Rise: 1370 meters (4500 ft)

Highlights: Mountain streams, First Purchase marker, view

Maps: USGS 7.5' Renovo East, Young Womans Creek, Slate Run, Oleona; Donut Hole Trail Maps 3 and 4

This hike uses parts of the Donut Hole and Susquehannock Trails to travel from Hyner Run to Ole Bull State Park. The latter is named for Ole Borneman Bull, a world-famous Norwegian violinist who in 1852 purchased 11,000 acres here in Potter County from an American swindler and proceeded to establish a settlement for Norwegian colonists. At that time Norway was one of the poorest countries in the world, and some 800 colonists moved here before the actual owner discovered the land ruse. He offered to sell his land to Bull at a low price but by then the tide had turned on the Norwegians' fortunes. Most of the colonists moved on to Wisconsin, but some stayed in Potter County and

their descendants live here today.

This hike requires a car shuttle. Leave one car at Ole Bull State Park on PA 144 a few miles south of its junction with PA 44 in Oleona. Check in with attendants at the park office for parking instructions. Then drive your second car south on PA 144 and turn left on PA 120 just west of Renovo. Continue east through Renovo and turn north to Hyner Run State Park in the village of Hyner. Total driving distance between the parks is 35.6 miles. Check in at the office at this end also for parking directions. For a camping permit call Sproul State Forest at 717-923-1450.

First Day
Hyner Run State Park to Bull Run
Distance: 18.3 km (11.4 miles)
Time: 7 hours

Pick up the Donut Hole Trail at a sign just beyond the park swimming pool, following red blazes up Log Road Hollow Trail. You soon pass a power-line swath, and then climb steadily and easily along the old road grade to a plateau. At 2.7 km turn right onto Fye Camp Trail and cross the Long Fork and its trail at 4 km. There is a spring about 150 meters to the left on

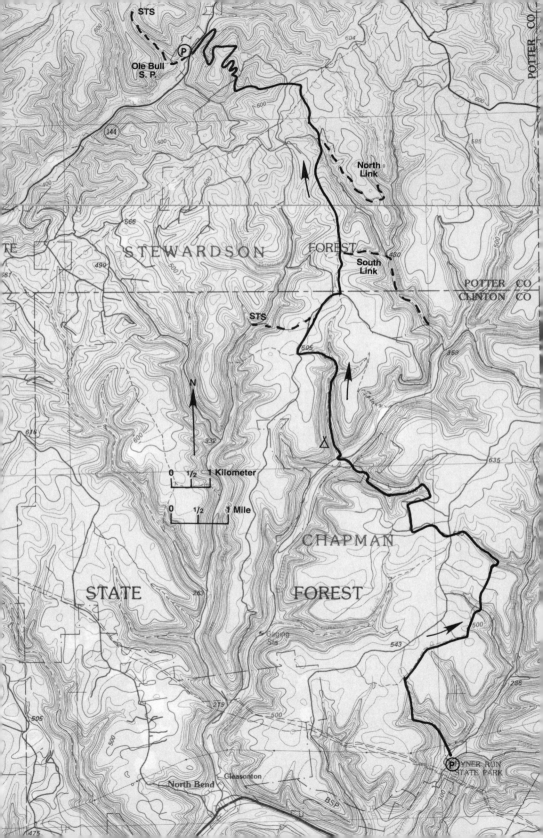

STS

Ole Bull
S. P.

144

North
Link

STEWARDSON   FOREST

South
Link

POTTER CO
CLINTON CO

STS

N

0   1/2   1 Kilometer

0   1/2   1 Mile

CHAPMAN

STATE   FOREST

Gaging
Sta

POTTER CO

North Bend

Gleasonton

BSP

YNER RUN
STATE PARK

this trail. Back on the Donut Hole Trail, you enter a large salvage cut; watch blazes carefully on this stretch. Shadbushes, a few maples, and occasional pines are the only trees the oak leaf roller has left alive. This area has been slow to recover.

Beyond the clear-cut you drop sharply to a tributary of Abe's Run and drop again to cross the run and Abe's Fork Road at 6.0 km. You then follow switch-backs up the far side to regain the plateau. At the next stream, descend on switchbacks and cross Cougar Run at 8.4 km. This name is a corruption of Koughler, a German immigrant and Civil War veteran who ran a trap line up this run in the last century.

Turn left up the run and pass a possible campsite at 8.8 km, where a side stream comes in from the right. Toward the top of Cougar Run turn left near a hunting camp and follows its access road across Dry Run Road at 10.0 km. Continue on Six Mile Road to 11.3 km; here you turn right on an obscure and poorly marked jeep road, but there is very little opportunity to turn anywhere else. At 12.4 km turn left onto a trail that descends to Seven Mile Run. At 14.8 km cross the run and bear left on Seven Mile Road; along this next stretch you walk past a piece of private land.

When you reach Young Woman's Creek, turn left to cross the stream via the road bridge. Young Woman's Creek is a famous trout stream. According to legend, the name stems from colonial times when a Native American, fearing approaching pursuers, killed a young woman whom he was holding captive at the creek's mouth. The young woman's ghost then haunted the area, reappearing whenever her killer returned to the creek. On a more positive note, a marker on your right, just beyond the bridge, commemorates the first purchase of state forest land back in 1898. Today state forests cover over 800,000 hectares.

Back on the trail, turn to your right in front of Bull Run hunting camp, cross Bull Run on a footbridge, and head upstream on an old grade. The grade soon gives out but the trail continues, mostly to the right of the stream. Good campsites lie along Bull Run; when you see one you like, set up your home for the night.

Second Day
Bull Run to Ole Bull State Park
Distance: 18.0 km (11.2 miles)
Time: 7 hours

In the morning continue up Bull Run. Turn left up a side stream at 19.1 km. You pass a trail register just before reaching Fork Hill Road. Turn right on the road and follow it to the orange-blazed Susquehannock Trail at 21.5 km, where Morgan Hollow Trail comes in on your left. Continue on Fork Hill Road to Rattlesnake Trail, where you turn left. This junction is fairly obscure. Moving along, you pass the blue-blazed Wildcat Trail on your right at 23.9 km. This is also known as the South Link Trail, and it heads east to the Black Forest Trail.

Rattlesnake Trail intersects Hartman Trail at 26.3 km; bear right along the edge of an impressive logging railroad cut to follow Hartman Trail down to Big Spring Branch. You walk along a number of old railroad grades and contemporary roads, so watch the blazes closely as you swing from one side of this valley to the other. At 27.6 km you pass the blue-blazed North Link Trail, which also leads east to the Black Forest Trail. Next is a springhouse with a stream of cold water, the first since Bull Run.

Now move through Spook Hollow, an evergreen plantation. At the top of the hollow turn left onto a jeep road, and then left again onto Twelve Mile Road at

29.6 km. After about 200 meters turn right onto Impson Hollow Trail. At 31.4 km turn right once more and follow switchbacks up to the plateau again. On the far side you descend to an overlook of Kettle Creek Valley, then move along switchbacks down to PA 144. Once you cross the highway and descend the bank, you're in Ole Bull State Park and near your car.

Free maps of the Donut Hole Trail and the relevant section of the Susquehannock Trail are available from Sproul State Forest, HCR 62, Box 90, Renovo, PA 17764.

48

Old Loggers Path

Distance: 44.7 km (27.8 miles)

Time: 3 days, 2 nights

Vertical Rise: 1020 meters (3340 ft)

Highlights: Views, waterfalls, ghost town

Maps: USGS 7.5' Barbours, Grover, Ralston, Bodines; Old Loggers Path map

The Old Loggers Path in Tiadaghton State Forest is an undiscovered gem of a Pennsylvania hiking trail. Thick woods, wild streams, and sweeping vistas give an illusion of remoteness to this wilderness trail, yet it is less than an hour's drive from Williamsport, the largest city in central Pennsylvania.

Pennsylvania has more ghost towns than Colorado. One of them is Masten, located on Pleasant Stream in northeastern Lycoming County. Hemlock and hardwood sawmills were opened around 1905 in Masten, which was on the standard-gauge Susquehanna and New York Railroad. In its early days Masten had a band and a baseball team. Six-room houses rented for $5 or $6 per month; running water was piped in from springs. There was one store in town. You weren't required to shop there, but where else could you go? Despite the isolation, people enjoyed themselves and maintained standards of a civilized life; for example, one night's entertainment, a medicine show, was so bad that the store's supply of eggs and vegetables was exhausted! Masten survived into the era of automobile and radio, thus ending a degree of isolation we would find difficult to comprehend. The last log was cut in 1930 and people moved away. A Civilian Conservation Corps camp moved in and stayed until 1940; the post office appears to have continued to serve the camp. Today only hunting camps remain.

The trailhead for the Old Loggers Path (OLP) is at Masten. It can be reached from PA 87 in Hillsgrove by driving Mill Creek Road for 9.4 miles. Much of this road follows the route of the narrow-gauge Susquehanna and Eagles Mere Railroad. You can also reach Masten from PA 14 at Marsh Hill by driving up Pleasant Stream Road for 9.3 miles, or from Ellenton, which you can reach from Shunk via PA 154. Once in Masten, park in the old CCC camp or in a wide spot in Pleasant Stream Road just above.

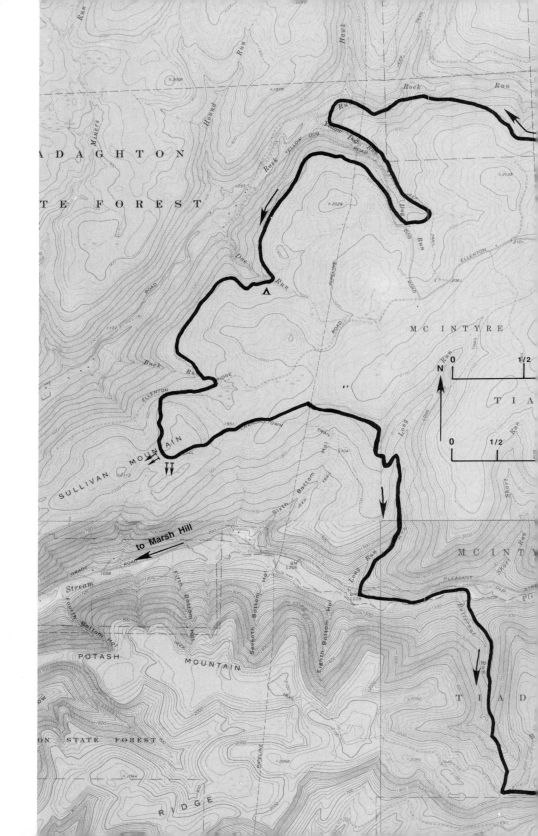

to Marsh Hill

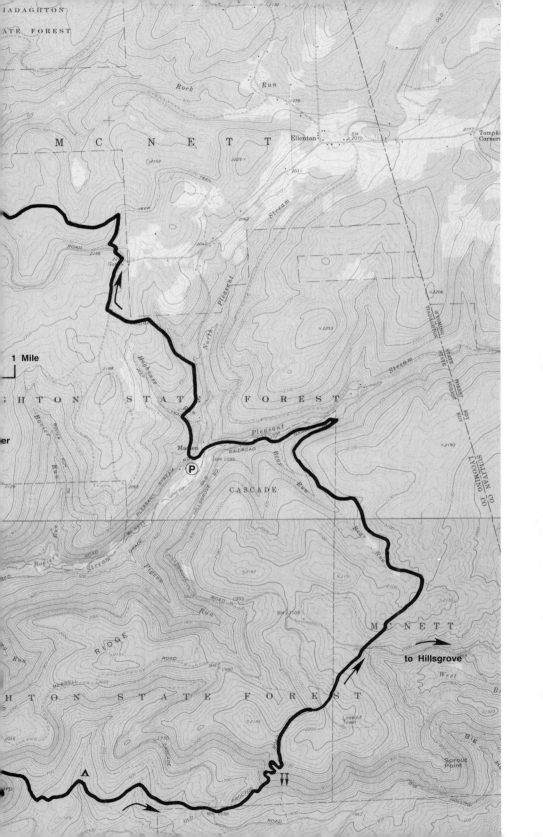

1 Mile

to Hillsgrove

The OLP is blazed orange. You will want your boots for this hike. Call Tiadaghton State Forest at 717-327-3450 for a camping permit.

First Day
Masten to Doe Run
Distance: 16.4 km (10.2 miles)
Time: 6 hours

Start your hike at the post sign and trail register along Pleasant Stream Road. There is a fallback campsite at Rock Run (10.4 km) so you don't have to make it all the way to Doe Run on this first day if you are running late—although of course you'll have to make up the distance tomorrow. The trail climbs away from Pleasant Stream on a series of old grades, passing a dry campsite at 0.8 km. Turn right at a trail sign and then turn right again on Kimm Road at 2.7 km. The blue blazes along this road mark it as part of a wintertime cross-country ski trail.

Pass a vehicle gate at 3.3 km and then bear left on Ellenton Ridge Road, which is open to cars. Shortly you bear right onto a trail, and then right again onto an old grade. Turn sharply left at 4.0 km in a clearing and follow an old logging railroad grade. Soon the trail crosses a clearing and then passes two junctions, with a blue-blazed ski trail to your right. The OLP descends gently, mostly on old grades, into Rock Run Valley.

Cross a pipeline swath and reach Rock Run campsite at 10.4 km. There are waterfalls and cascades in Rock Run. This is a possible campsite but there is a road of sorts—passable to vehicles—on the other side of the stream.

Turn left and climb gently on a grade, recrossing the pipeline swath. Near the top you cross two streams and then bear right on Yellow Dog Road at 12.8 km. Shortly you bear left on a logging rail-road grade (Stoney Trail), passing a trail register. Please sign in. The footway development of the OLP indicates that usage is about a factor of ten greater than the number registered. The footway is obvious to people in the field but those in offices, who allocate resources, see only the number registered.

The trail continues along the edge of Ellenton Ridge, crossing a small stream and the pipeline again. At 16.4 km you cross Doe Run, a larger stream. Campsites for your first night are found on the far side of Doe Run.

Second Day
Doe Run to Wallis Run
Distance: 16.7 km (10.4 miles)
Time: 6 hours

Today the trail continues along the edge of Ellenton Ridge, passing some large rocks. Turn right on Ellenton Ridge Road, usually gated off to traffic at this point. Immediately cross Buck Run. Proceed past the gated Crandall Town Trail to 19.3 km where you turn left on trail. This turn is followed by a steep climb that brings you to the top of Sullivan Mountain and an extensive view to the west. Then continue around Sullivan Mountain for another view to the south. Continue over more ledges and then descend steeply on trail to a junction of woods roads at 21.2 km. Turn half-right on the Crandall Town Road; avoid the road to your extreme right.

At 22.4 km you cross the pipeline for the last time and continue ahead on a recent trail relocation. The relocation follows a ridge between Sixth Bottom Hollow and Long Run. It then switchbacks down the east side of the ridge and crosses Long Run. Turn right at 24.6 km, and follow a rough grade downstream. Cross Long Run again and reach Pleasant Stream Road at 26.2 km.

Turn left and cross Long Run on the road bridge. Then turn right and left again on the Susquehanna and New York Railroad grade. At 27.6 km turn right off the S & NY, soon reaching Pleasant Stream itself. Cross as best you can, for there is no bridge. Next you begin to climb along Butternut Run on an old logging road that evaporates near the top. Cross Merrell Road and follow another recent trail relocation along the south edge of Burnetts Ridge.

Bear right on a road at the end of the relocation to reach Sharp Top Vista at 31.3 km. In front of you the world drops away to reveal a broad wooded valley, surrounded by mountains. The geologic structure may resemble that of Nippenose and Sugar Valleys in the ridge-and-valley region—but this is the Allegheny Plateau. Across from you is a prominent water gap between Cove and Camp Mountains that cuts through the ridge from Proctor to Barbours. Only a few buildings are visible in the valley. The rampart of Burnetts Ridge stretches off to the west. I find it hard to understand why this view isn't famous.

When you feel you must move on, find the trail, leaving the far side of the turnaround. Follow it downhill to 32.9 km where you turn left on a logging road. Soon you reach a good campsite at the crossing of the east branch of Wallis Run. Camp on either side of the run.

Third Day
Wallis Run to Masten
Distance: 11.6 km (7.2 miles)
Time: 4½ hours

Today you continue along the base of Burnetts Ridge on a series of old roads and trails. You cross several more streams but none offer as good a campsite as the one on Wallis Run. At 35.3 km cross Cascade Road and start to climb on the Old Proctor Road Trail. Near the top is a blue-blazed side trail to your right that leads to Sprout Point Vista—a reprise of yesterday's view from Sharp Top.

After returning from the vista, turn right and complete the climb. On the top you cross a forestry road and continue on Old Proctor Road, which takes you downhill past a hunting camp to Hillsgrove Road at 38.6 km. Jog left across the road and continue on the trail, which soon crosses a grassy logging road. Continue along the broad top of Burnetts Ridge and then gradually swing left onto an old railroad grade that leads down Bear Run. At 41.2 km you cross a couple of small streams that provide the only water along this section. Avoid an obvious trail that diverges left at 42.1 km, and continue ahead on the railroad grade. The railroad grade now swings east up the Pleasant Stream valley. Next turn left off the grade and drop down to the Susquehanna and New York Railroad grade, where you turn left. Continue over Bear Run and then turn right through an evergreen plantation with a trail register. Then swing left behind the hunting camp and bear left on the road past some more hunting camps. Keep right at the junction with the Hillsgrove Road and follow the road over Pleasant Stream and North Pleasant Stream to your car.

A free map of the Old Loggers Path can be obtained by writing Tiadaghton State Forest, 423 East Central Avenue, South Williamsport, PA 17701. The Keystone Trails Association sells an Old Loggers Path patch for $3.50 (including sales tax and postage). Write to PO Box 251, Cogan Station, PA 17728-0251.

49

Mid State Trail

Distance: 44.7 km (27.8 miles)

Time: 3 days, 2 nights

Vertical Rise: 1530 meters (5020 ft)

Highlights: Views, tunnel

Maps: USGS 7.5' Hartleton, Woodward, Weikert, Coburn; MSTA Maps 205, 206, & 207

Bald Eagle State Forest, which at 78,000 hectares is one of Pennsylvania's largest, is the setting for this hike. The gypsy moth appeared in this area in the early 1970s, and, without any natural enemies, began defoliating the oak forests. Many oaks died as a result; at several points along this hike you will see salvage cuts where dead oaks were logged, mostly for pulpwood.

This hike crosses Bald Eagle State Forest on the Mid State Trail, roughly following the eastern boundary of Centre County. The forest is named for a Native American chief whose village was located on Bald Eagle Creek in the early 1800s. You will walk the only foot trail in the Commonwealth that tunnels under a mountain rather than forcing you to climb over it.

You need a car shuttle for this hike. First drive to R.B. Winter State Park on PA 192. Check in at the park office for parking directions and leave one car here. In your other car drive west on PA 192 through Livonia and Rebersburg. Then turn left on PA 445 and go through the Millheim Narrows. Turn right on PA 45 at the only traffic light in Millheim and drive west to a sign for Poe Valley State Park. Turn left here and then left again on Penns Creek Road. After passing Rotes Mill turn right on the Millheim-Siglerville Turnpike and follow it to Big Poe Valley. Turn left on Big Poe Road to Poe Valley State Park. Check in the park office for parking instructions. You will want your hiking boots for the notoriously rocky Mid State Trail. For a camping permit call Bald Eagle State Forest at 717-922-3344.

First Day
Poe Valley State Park to Libby Run
Distance: 15.4 km (9.6 miles)
Time: 6 hours

Start your hike on the blue-blazed Hunters Path that begins at the water pump next to the concession stand. Follow the Hunters Path up the steep flank of Little Poe Mountain to a junction with the orange-blazed Mid State Trail (MST) at the top of the ridge. Turn left on the Thorpe Trail and follow it along the crest of Little Poe Mountain. This trail was cut by the Penn State Outing Club in 1979 and is named for State Forester Richard Thorpe, who originally suggested this route for the Mid State Trail. Little Poe Mountain consists of Bald Eagle sandstone of Ordovician age. This layer fractures into large tabular blocks and makes a better footway than the Lower Silurian Tuscarora quartzite; however, the Bald Eagle has more water gaps that have to be crossed.

You soon reach one of these gaps and descend steeply to cross Little Poe Road and Creek at 3.3 km. Beyond the creek you climb up the Dry Hollow Trail to a trail register at the height-of-land. The Mid State Trail turns right here and climbs to the top of Long Mountain. (In wet or slippery weather continue ahead on the blue-blazed Dry Hollow Trail to Big Poe Road and bear right to Poe Paddy State Park, where you rejoin the Mid State Trail.) Along the crest of Long Mountain you pass a view across Panther Hollow at the top of a cliff. Next you reach the Jump Off, where you descend steeply on rocky footway. As you near the end of Long Mountain, you pass another view of High Mountain. Just beyond, you reach a view east down Penns Creek flanked by Paddy and White Mountains.

You then descend steeply to Poe Paddy State Park at the junction of Swift Run and Big Poe Roads and Poe Paddy Drive at 6.6 km. Continue ahead on Poe Paddy Drive, crossing Big Poe Creek and bearing right on an unnamed road which takes you past one of the sites of the ghost town of Poe's Mills. After traversing a stretch of private land, turn right on the abandoned Penn Central Railroad grade. Cross Penns Creek on the old railroad trestle and continue under Paddy Mountain via the 85-meter tunnel.

On the far side of Paddy Mountain you follow the Penn Central Railroad grade east to a recent trail relocation around private land. Turn left and follow new trail to a corner of the private land. Then turn right, descend to Cherry Run, and cross it on a footbridge behind a hunting camp. Turn left on Cherry Run Road and follow it through a gap in Paddy Mountain. Next, turn left on Old Mingle Road for 300 meters; then turn right and follow the Mid State Trail through the gap between Sawmill Mountain and First Green Knob. Your camp for the night is at the crossing of Libby Run.

Second Day
Libby Run to Buffalo Creek
Distance: 16.2 km (10.1 miles)
Time: 7 hours

Your hike today is more demanding so you'll want to get an early start. First you continue up Libby Hollow to Rupp Hollow Road. Beyond, you follow an old wagon road up the south flank of Thick Mountain. Next you cross the flat top of the mountain to an overlook of the east end of Penns Valley, and then swing south to a junction with the Bear Run Trail. At 20.0 km you turn left on the Rock Knob Trail and follow it to the base of Rock Knob itself. Turn right and climb over Rock Knob. There is an extensive view to the south, and by climbing onto a low tree branch you can also get a view north to Winkelblech Mountain. You descend the north flank of Thick Mountain on an old log skid and cross Woodward Gap Road at Johnson Spring. Johnson Spring provides water

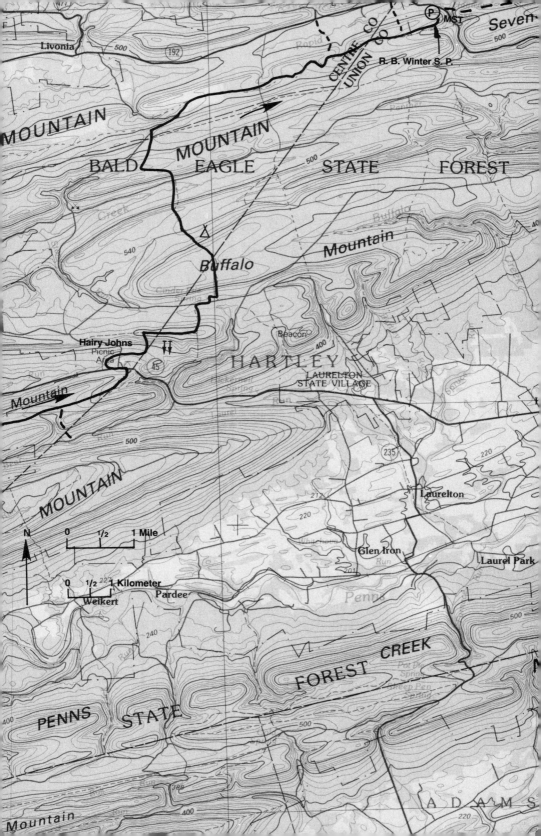

at 8 degrees C on hot summer days and may be the coldest spring on the Mid State Trail. There is another spring to the left just past the gate.

Beyond Woodward Gap Road you follow the Sand Hollow Trail east past a gypsy moth salvage cut. More salvage cutting is underway in Sand Hollow, but any trees still alive are to be left along the Mid State Trail. At 24.7 km you reach an intersection with the blue-blazed Bear Gap Trail. This trail leads right to a campsite and spring. Back on the main trail you proceed east, and after passing a trail register you bear left over Sand Mountain to PA 45 and Hairy Johns State Forest Picnic Area.

Cross the highway and follow the orange blazes through the picnic area. Hairy John Vonida was an unshaven hermit who lived here in the 19th century along the old stage road into Centre County after his family died in an epidemic. He would bring spring water to the passengers on the stagecoach but would not speak to anyone. Before PA 45 was a stage road, it was the Penns Creek Indian Path.

After passing a small pond fed by Hairy Johns Spring, you bear left on the Hairy Johns Trail through open woods to the base of Winkelblech Mountain. Climb the steep south flank on rough trail to a view south near the top of the ridge. At the top turn right on the Winkelblech Trail. Do the rock ledges look familiar? This is the same Bald Eagle sandstone that forms Little Poe Mountain.

Next you turn left on the Sheesley Hollow Trail. Note the foundations of an aircraft navigation beacon just beyond this junction. Pennsylvania's ridges are not very high but they have collected more than their share of airplane wreckage over the years. After descending the north side of the ridge you turn right on the Bucknell Outing Club Trail and cross both branches of Sheesley Run. Then

bear right on Stony Run Road and pass Cinder Pile Spring. Geared locomotives of the Laurelton Lumber Company offloaded cinders here as they refilled their water tanks from the spring. If you suspect Buffalo Creek is dry, fill your canteen, pots, and water bag at Cinder Pile Spring.

At 30.5 km you turn left on the Kessler Trail and climb the south flank of Buffalo Mountain. Tonight's campsite is just north of Buffalo Creek, to the right of the trail. This creek is fed by swamps to the west and its tea-colored water flows most of the year.

Third Day
Buffalo Creek to R.B. Winter State Park
Distance: 13.0 km (8.1 miles)
Time: 5 hours

This morning your path takes you across the grain of the ridge-and-valley region, descending Buffalo and then Sharpback Mountain. On the bench between these ridges you cross Negro Hollow Road, named for a black man who ran a logging camp a bit east of here. There is a walled spring to the right of the trail, 200 meters beyond the road. Down Sharpback the trail passes through a dense stand of evergreens. Next you cross Centre County's Pine Creek (not to be confused with Pine Creek in Lycoming County) and then Pine Creek Road at 34.2 km. Continue on the Wise Trail, which slabs up the south side of Buck Ridge.

Next you turn right on the Hairy Johns Trail and cross Panther Run. Just beyond, you cross another old logging railroad grade of the Laurelton Lumber Company. At the top of Shriner Mountain you cross Fallen Timber Trail and then turn right on the Stover Gap Road. (Horse Path Spring is 20 meters straight

Tunnel under Paddy Mountain

ahead near the hunting camp.) At the switchback on Stover Gap Road continue ahead on the logging railroad grade, which emerges from under the road. You then traverse a seed tree cut that has abundant blueberries in early July.

Beyond the seed tree cut you continue on the Brush Hollow Trail, passing junctions with the Fallen Shriner, Douty Mill, Oley Camp, and West Link Trails. Next cross Yankee Run Trail. Just 260 meters beyond Yankee Run Trail you cross the outlet from Crocodile Spring.

You pass Long Trail on the left and at 43.4 km you reach a major trail junction at the west end of R.B. Winter State Park. Avoid the West Boundary Trail, which goes left over Brush Mountain to PA 192, and the blue-blazed East Link cross-country ski trail, which goes right over Shriner Mountain. Continue ahead along the park boundary and then turn left through an evergreen plantation above Rapid Run. You emerge on PA 192 at the highway bridge over Rapid Run. Just beyond is Halfway Dam and the pond that forms the heart of R.B. Winter State Park. On the far side the beach beckons you for a swim in the spring-fed waters.

The Mid State Trail map and guide set can be mail-ordered from Mid State Trail Association, PO Box 167, Boalsburg, PA 16827. Write for the current price.

50

Quehanna Trail

Distance: 116.6 km (72.5 miles)

Time: 7 days, 6 nights

Vertical Rise: 2625 meters (8610 ft)

Highlights: Quehanna Wild Area

Maps: USGS 7.5' Huntley, Weedville, Dents Run, Driftwood, Devils Elbow, The Knobs, Sinnemahoning, Penfield; USGS 1:100,000 Clearfield; Quehanna Trail, western and eastern sections

The Quehanna's wild and beautiful country offers you a real challenge even if you're an experienced backpacker. For 54 km the trail traverses the Quehanna Wild Area, Pennsylvania's largest such preserve, and it also passes through the Marion Brooks Natural Area. Along the way you are likely to see a profusion of wildlife, including fox, beaver, and the abundant deer. The largest bear I have seen outside a zoo was on the Quehanna.

Opened in 1976, this loop trail is only now beginning to attract the use it merits. Today there is frequently a trace of footway to lead you between the blazes. Don't try the Quehanna until you've completed a couple of backpacking trips. However, if you wish to try part of the trail, three blue-blazed connectors form shorter loops of about 11, 28, and 79 km.

There have been a number of trail relocations since 1977, reducing road and pipeline walking and taking the trail past more springs and views. Another relocation avoids the damage caused by the tornado of May 1985. Quehanna Trail maps may be obtained by writing to Moshannon State Forest, PO Box 952, Clearfield, PA 16830; or to Elk State Forest, RD #1, Route 155, Box 327, Emporium, PA 15834. Call 814-765-3741 for a camping permit.

The Quehanna Trail's backpacking rules prohibit camping in the state game lands, Marion Brooks Natural Area, and within 100 meters of a drivable road. You should not camp more than 2 consecutive nights at any one site, and groups are limited to six persons. You may obtain exemption to this limit by applying to the Moshannon or Elk Forest offices in advance. Be extremely careful with fires as the area has been devastated by both the oak leaf roller and the gypsy moth, and dead trees abound. A small backpacking stove presents a minimal fire hazard.

To reach the trailhead in Parker Dam State Park, take Exit 18 off I-80, drive north on PA 153 for 5.1 miles, and turn right on Mud Run Road for 2.4 miles to the park office. Check in and follow the campground road to the large signboard at the trailhead.

First Day
Parker Dam State Park to Deer Creek
Distance: 20.9 km (13.0 miles)
Time: 8 hours

At the map board, head up the orange-blazed Log Slide Trail. A small part of the slide is reconstructed here. Cross a couple of pipelines, jog right on the CPL Trail, and resume hiking up Little Laurel Run. CPL stands for Central Pennsylvania Lumber Company, which in the early 1900s was the logging subsidiary of the United States Leather Company. Tannic acid obtained from hemlock bark was used to tan the prodigious amounts of leather required when horses were still a primary means of travel and machinery was run by belts instead of electric motors.

At 4.0 km jog left on Laurel Run Road. You soon recross it, then cross Tyler Road and an extensive meadow where you are likely to see deer. Shortly the blue-blazed Cut Off Trail goes off to your left. At 7.0 km you arrive at the junction of McGeorge and Wallace Mine Roads. Bear left on a new trail that parallels Wallace Mine Road. Then recross Wallace Mine Road. The blue-blazed West Cross Connector turns left on Wallace Mine Road. Follow new trail to a crossing of the Alex Branch. Next, turn left along the Alex Branch and cross it a second time, returning to the old trail. At 9.8 km, climb away from the Alex Branch to avoid private land and soon enter State Game Land (SGL) 94. At 11.2 km

you reach a pipeline. Drop your pack here and walk ahead about 100 meters for a view across Trout Run.

Back on the trail, follow the pipeline swath down and across Trout Run to an old railroad grade. Then turn right, and swing around east into Roberts Run. The grade disappears. You keep to the left of the run and pass among large sandstone boulders. At 14.1 km leave the game lands and turn right on a relocation, crossing Roberts Run. Circle through a side valley and then return to the old trail at the spring just south of Roberts Run (a possible campsite if it's getting late). Next follow another side valley south to the top of Chestnut Ridge before proceeding east to cross Knobs Ridge Road at 18.8 km. Continue east into the headwaters of Deer Creek, crossing it near a spring. Camp between the spring and the forks of Deer Creek.

Second Day
Deer Creek to Twelve Mile Run
Distance: 18.4 km (11.4 miles)
Time: 8 hours

Continue on trail now going upstream along the other fork of Deer Creek to the Caledonia Pike. Jog right on the pike and follow the road to Mineral Springs Camp. Then bear right on trail at an obscure turn and proceed to a bridge over Gifford Run at 23.4 km. On the far side, head downstream, crossing a side stream at 24.1 km and a larger one at 25.9 km. Next, climb to a view across Gifford Run and continue on trail to Merrill Road at 27.3 km. Then turn left on a jeep road and soon bear right on a very obscure relocation which leads you to Deserter Run, just inside the Quehanna Wild Area. Turn upstream and then bear right on a woods road at 29.2 km. Next pass under a large power line and continue to 31.2 km; turn right along the white-blazed border of State Game Land 34. Next cross Lost Run Road—where the blue-blazed East Cross Connector Trail goes left—and continue on new trail to the edge of Mosquito Creek Valley.

Turn right and bushwhack along the edge. Do not follow the orange blazes down into the rhododendron. No side hill construction has been completed here, nor has the overhead been cleared for hikers with packs. Occasionally you will see blazes below you. At 32.7 km you rejoin the blazes briefly where they cross a power line; rejoin them again at 33.5 km for Panther Run Vista. Beyond the vista the trail again goes over the valley's side, but you soon pick it up. Turn right on it as it heads away from the edge. At 33.8 km the trail turns left. Jog left across another power line. The trail continues along the ridge between Lost Run and Mosquito Creek, passing a white birch grove and then a freestanding rock. At the brink of the final cliffs, bear right and then, at the base, cut left to continue past a hunting camp. You cross Mosquito Creek on a swing bridge at 38.8 km. Turn right for the short distance to Twelve Mile Run, whose water is better than the Mosquito's for drinking. The best camp-sites are on the far side of the run, which you cross on a cable bridge.

Third Day
Twelve Mile Run to Big Spring Draft
Distance: 18.5 km (11.5 miles)
Time: 7 hours

This is a shorter day after yesterday's big push. Look around at this meadow you camped in. Why isn't this valley V-shaped like all the others? Just before you turn and climb out of the valley, you see large piles of rocks marking the meadow's downstream end. These piles are the ruins of Corporation Dam, a splash dam built in the last century, that blocked Gifford Run, Mosquito Creek, and Twelve Mile Run. The meadow formed as the dam filled with sand and silt. Eventually Mosquito Creek cut through the dam and carved a minicanyon through the meadow. Notice that the stumps along Mosquito Creek are at the level of the original land surface, considerably below the meadow's surface. Such is the fate of all dams.

Your climb out of Mosquito Creek Valley is the first real one on the trail. Just opposite those piles of stones, turn sharply left and follow an old wagon road past House Rock to the summit. Proceed along trail to 41.8 km, where you cross under a power line and continue on a woods road. You then follow a series of woods roads, passing unmarked springs at 42.5 and 44.5 km. Turn left onto trail at 45.9 km. Then cross Cole Run and continue upstream along Fisher Rocks Branch past a spring to the Quehanna Highway at 47.9 km.

Cross the highway and follow the trail through a thick stand of maple saplings. Then pass a spring, which would make a good campsite if you are running late. Cross a power line at 49.4 km and traverse an old burn area with some views of the plateau. Turn left in the burn area and reenter the woods crossing a logging road, a power line, and a woods road. Then descend and continue on an old logging road, passing a number of spring seeps. Follow the old logging road as it swings west around the side of the hill. Where the old road swings south watch closely for a right turn onto trail that drops down to a forestry road. Follow the road downhill across Upper Three Runs, bear left on Old Sinnemahoning Road (which has reverted to trail), and climb

Cable bridge over Twelve Mile Run

gently back to the plateau where you bear left on (new) Sinnemahoning Road at 55.5 km. Along this stretch of road you pass several blue-blazed cross-country ski trails and cross into the 1985 tornado zone. At 57.1 km the blue-blazed Big Spring Draft takes off to the left. The Big Spring itself is just below but not visible from the road. It is the only water between Upper Three Runs and Upper Pine Hollow. Camp here but get out of sight of the road.

Fourth Day
Big Spring Draft to Arch Spring
Distance: 14.3 km (8.9 miles)
Time: 5½ hours

Immediately beyond Big Spring Draft continue ahead on the old Sinnemahoning Trail where it diverges from the modern road. Then bear left on a drivable road. Continue under a power line and reach a critical turn at 61.0 km. This turn is at last marked with a post sign. Note the bear bites on this sign. (If you miss this important turn you soon come to a pipeline swath.) Turn left onto trail.

Then follow the footway past the site of a hunting camp and into a draw which leads into Upper Pine Hollow. At 63.1 km Upper Pine Draft comes in from the left and provides a campsite for a small party. Toward the bottom of the hollow cross Pine Draft Run as best you can. There is a footbridge across Wykoff Run. Then make your way out to Wykoff Road and bear right. Cross Laurel Run on the highway bridge and turn left at 63.2 km. There are only two crossings of the run and they can be avoided by keeping right. You pass a spring to the left at 64.6 km. At the top of the climb you enter a meadow. There is another spring just before the bridge over Laurel Draft at the far side of the meadow. Then cross a couple of pipelines, a

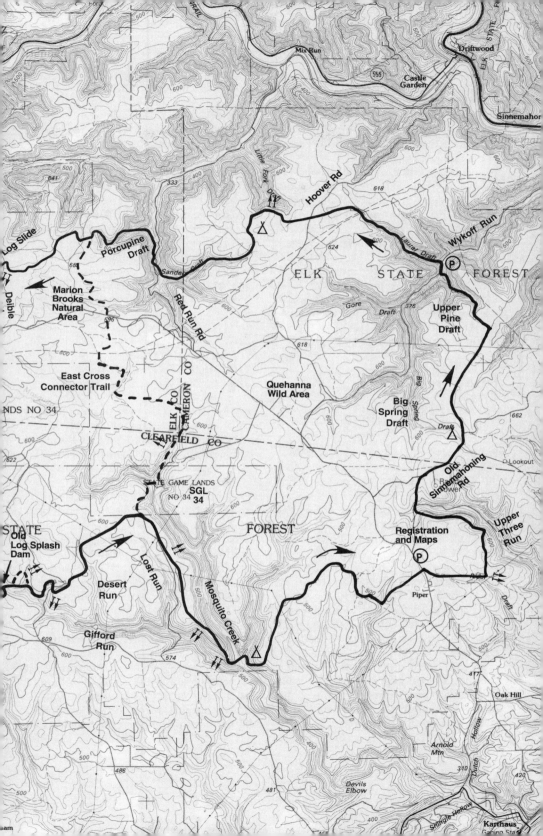

power line, and then the draft again, to go past several beaver dams. You pass a spring on your left at 68.3 km. Just beyond you pass the only trailside shelter on the Quehanna Trail—dirt floor and leaky roof. Still, the nearby spring makes this a fallback campsite.

After the shelter, watch for an obscure spot where the trail bears left off a woods road. Next you cross Hoover Road at 69.3 km; continue down a woods road to a small meadow; cross an intermittent stream; and bear right on trail. You next pass through a grove of white birch and at 71.2 km you reach the best view on the Quehanna Trail. The view looks down Little Fork Draft to Mix Run and is worth a lengthy stop. Back on the trail you pass Arch Spring at 71.6 km. Camp at the top of the slope, just beyond Arch Spring.

Fifth Day
Arch Spring to Mix Run
Distance: 17.7 km (11.0 miles)
Time: 8 hours

Follow the jeep road out to a road junction where you go straight into the woods and follow Sanders Draft. Soon you cross to the other side of the stream. The trail crosses repeatedly before reaching the forks of Sanders Draft (a possible campsite) at 75.7 km. Continue downstream and cross Red Run on a pole bridge. Then bear right on Red Run Road. Turn left up Porcupine Draft, just before the road bridge over Red Run. You follow an old railroad grade at first, but it soon gives out and you continue climbing among large boulders in this miniature glen. Continue climbing to the top of Porcupine Draft. Here you go through open woods and then jog left on Losey Road. The blue-blazed East Cross Connector Trail comes up from the south along this road.

Make your way through a rock garden

to a spring at the head of Mud Lick Hollow. Here the Quehanna Trail turns south, crossing a forestry road, and enters the Marion Brooks Natural Area at 83.1 km. Turn right where the blue-blazed High Water Route goes straight. Cross Deible Road at the far side of the Natural Area and follow the trail to a vista across Deible Run. Then descend to a low-water crossing of Deible Run. Turn right onto old trail. At 87.5 km you reach Mix Run and turn upstream. Cross a series of three footbridges over Mix Run, designed by Ralph Seeley and built by the Keystone Trails Association's Trail Care Project and Pennsylvania Conservation Corps. Camp after the third bridge.

Sixth Day
Mix Run to Bear Run
Distance: 14.1 km (8.8 miles)
Time: 6½ hours

Tom Mix, the cowboy star of silent films, was born downstream where Mix Run meets Bennett Branch. However, his official biography moved his birthplace to El Paso, Texas, for professional reasons.

Your hike today takes you upstream along Mix Run past Camp Hide Out. Cross Mix Run on a bridge and bear right, avoiding the grade up the side of the valley, and continue upstream. Cross two pipelines and then Grant Road at 91.9 km. Then cross two more pipelines, a couple of streams, and another pipeline, to reach the white-blazed boundary of State Game Land 34. Continue down Silver Mill Hollow, reenter state forest land, cross the stream, and then turn left at an obscure turn at 96.4 km. Then pick up a dug footway that slabs the hillside. At 99.3 km, after crossing several pipelines and under a power line, you cross the Quehanna Highway and Sullivan Run and pick up the dug footway again. Follow it to a crossing of the Medix Grade Road, and turn downstream to a new footbridge over Medix Run. This bridge, designed by Gert Aron, was also built by the Trail Care Project of the Keystone Trails Association along with the Pennsylvania Conservation Corps. Next you turn left and climb up Bear Run. There is usually still some water near the last crossing of Bear Run. Camp as soon as you reach the level area above Bear Run. Despite what the Quehanna Trail Map says, there is no view.

Seventh Day
Bear Run to Parker Dam State Park
Distance: 13.9 km (8.6 miles)
Time: 5 hours

From camp you follow trail through the woods to the Caledonia Pike at 103.9 km. Continue through the woods past a view and then descend to the crossing of a branch of Laurel Run. Next, turn left up Laurel Run, following an old road. At 109.3 km bear left on Saunders Road; just around the bend the blue-blazed West Cross Connector Trail comes in from the left. Continue to a grassy road just beyond a piped spring on your left at 110.8 km and bear right. Follow an old road grade up Big Saunders Run and cross on a footbridge.

Cross a side stream and then turn right on a recent trail relocation. Climb steeply out of the valley and the enter a tornado salvage cut. Here you pick up a logging road. Then bear left on a better log road and cross Tyler Road at 114.7 km. Follow an old road around a gate and under a power line. The blue-blazed Cut Off Trail comes in at 115.8 km and you reenter civilization at the campground RV dump station. Continue ahead on the paved road to the map board where you set out 1 week ago.

Books from The Countryman Press and Backcountry Publications

The Countryman Press and Backcountry Publications, long known for fine books on travel and outdoor recreation, offer a range of practical and readable manuals.

Hiking Series

Fifty Hikes in the Adirondacks
Fifty Hikes in Central New York
Fifty Hikes in Central Pennsylvania
Fifty Hikes in Connecticut
Fifty Hikes in Eastern Pennsylvania
Fifty Hikes in the Hudson Valley
Fifty Hikes in Lower Michigan
Fifty Hikes in Massachusetts
Fifty Hikes in New Jersey
Fifty Hikes in the Mountains of North Carolina
Fifty Hikes in Northern Maine
Fifty Hikes in Northern Virginia
Fifty Hikes in Ohio
Fifty Hikes in Southern Maine
Fifty Hikes in Vermont
Fifty Hikes in Western New York
Fifty Hikes in Western Pennsylvania
Fifty Hikes in the White Mountains
Fifty More Hikes in New Hampshire

Walks & Rambles Series

Walks & Rambles in Dutchess and Putnam Counties
Walks & Rambles in Rhode Island, 2nd Ed.
More Walks & Rambles in Rhode Island
Walks & Rambles in Southwestern Ohio
Walks & Rambles in Westchester & Fairfield Counties, 2nd Ed.
Walks & Rambles in the Upper Connecticut River Valley
Walks & Rambles on Cape Cod and the Islands
Walks & Rambles on the Delmarva Peninsula
Walks & Rambles in and around St. Louis

We offer many more books on hiking, walking, fishing, and canoeing, plus books on travel, nature, and many other subjects. Our books are available through bookstores or directly from the publisher. For ordering information or for a complete catalog, please contact: The Countryman Press, c/o W.W. Norton & Company, Inc., 800 Keystone Industrial Park, Scranton, PA 18512 http:web.wwnorton.com